Claudio Arrau

London 1980

Jerrold Northrop Moore

ELGAR *A Life in Photographs*

London · Oxford University Press · 1972

ELGAR *A Life in Photographs*

Worcester in 1792, seen from the north-west.
The surrounding landscape has probably been
idealized by the artist, but this was how the
residents liked to think of their city far into
the nineteenth century.

Worcester about 1860, as it was during Elgar's childhood.

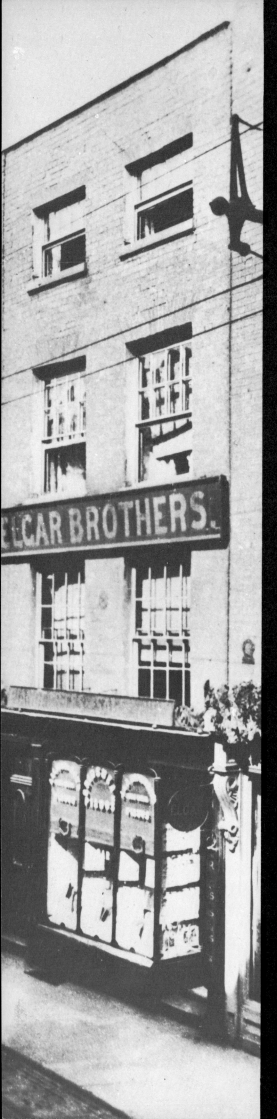

William Henry Elgar (1821-1906). A native of Dover with a
London music shop apprenticeship, he came to Worcester in
1841 as an itinerant piano tuner. There he found lodgings with
a family called Greening, and in 1848 he married Mr. Greening's
sister Anne. Seven children were born to them. Together with
his brother Henry, Elgar founded his own music shop in
Worcester at no. 10, High Street in 1860, and shortly afterward
brought his growing family to live above the shop.

W. H. Elgar played the violin well enough to find himself in
demand amongst the city's various musical groups. He was also
organist of St. George's Catholic Church, though he himself
did not join the Church until old age. One member of the choir
remembered him thus:

*Old E. always handed round the snuff-box before commencing
the mass, 'damned' the blower, and began. Went out at sermon
for drink at Hop Market.*

Elgar Bros. Music Shop, No. 10, High Street, Worcester.
All the Elgar children grew up in the family home above the shop,
and all took their turns at serving its customers. As late as 1896,
when Edward's *The Light of Life* was being produced at the
Three Choirs Festival in Worcester, a Festival visitor entering
the shop was startled to find the composer himself behind the
counter. One of Edward's letters about a pet dog evokes the
atmosphere:

*I shut him up at the shop this morn: while I went to give a
lesson, he whined so [my mother] let him out, he darted down
the stairs, caught his leg in twenty concertinas that are piled
on the staircase & rolled over with all the lot into the middle
of the shop! There were some ladies there & my old father
enjoyed it awfully.*

Only a sprig of heather
    But it grew upon the wild
When you and I together
    The summer day beguiled.
When the skylark high was singing
    Above the yellow broom
And the cool hill-breeze was bringing
    The sweet scent of its bloom.

Anne Elgar on a visit to
Old Hills, July 1878.

Anne Greening Elgar (1822-1902). The daughter of a
Gloucestershire yeoman farmer, she grew up in her childhood
home near the Forest of Dean. She was a great reader, wrote
poetry throughout her life, and saw to it that each of her
children was well educated by her own standard. Shortly after
her marriage she became a convert to Roman Catholicism.
Her eldest daughter remembered:

*Our Mother was romantic by temperament, and poetic by
nature. She had the unmistakable air of good breeding . . . Her
very soul was wrapped up in her husband and children.
She often drove out with Father in the country on his business
tours, and while he was occupied she would sketch the churches
and little bits of pleasing scenery . . .*

*Three of us, Harry, myself, and Polly had been born within
the shadow of our dear Cathedral but my Mother's wish for
country life prompted Father to go to Broadheath . . .*

7

The Malvern Hills to the west of Worcester. Rising up suddenly from
the Vale of Evesham, the Hills dominate the surrounding countryside.
Much of Edward's music was to be conceived and set down within
sight of the Malverns.

*How well I remember the day he was born. The air
was sweet with the perfume of flowers, bees were
humming and all the earth was lovely. There seemed
to us little ones to be a lot of unnecessary running
about in the house, and Father came tearing up the
drive with a strange man in a carriage . . . we were
taken a scamper across the heath to be out of the way.*

LUCY ELGAR   *1912*

The rural home the Elgars found in 1856 was a
cottage at Broadheath, in the countryside to
the north-west of Worcester and just beyond
the northern end of the Malverns. In a tiny
first floor bedroom at the left rear Edward was
born on 2 June 1857.

Edward and his mother, 1859.

Shortly before 1860 the exigencies of the Elgar business forced the family to give up the Broadheath idyll and return to Worcester to live above the shop. Thus Edward was the only one of their children to be born outside the city.

High Street, Worcester, looking toward the Cathedral. The Elgar sign hangs in front of the shop, the third building on the left.

. . . I saw and learnt a great deal about music from the stream of music that passed through my father's establishment . . . I read everything, played everything, and heard everything that I possibly could.

EDWARD ELGAR   1904

One of Edward's abiding childhood memories was the way he took to school with his closest chum, Hubert Leicester:

. . . Our walk was always to the brightly-lit west. Before starting, our finances were rigidly inspected . . . The report being favourable, two pence were 'allowed' for the ferry. Descending the steps, past the door behind which the figure of the mythical salmon is incised, we embarked; at our backs 'the unthrift sun shot vital gold', filling Payne's Meadows with glory and illuminating for two small boys a world to conquer and to love.

The Elgar children

In 1874 Mrs. Elgar wrote a couplet on each of her surviving children.

Dainty, little dainty girl
Fit to sit in gold or pearl.

Mirthful, saucy, singing lass
Greets you gaily as you pass.

Henry John (1850-1864).
'Harry' showed early signs of musical promise, but died of scarlet fever before he was fourteen, leaving Edward the eldest son.

Lucy Ann (1852-1925).
A clever, impetuous girl, she married a young Worcester merchant. In old age Lucy became stone deaf and rather a recluse.

Susanna Mary (1855-1936).
'Polly' was Edward's favourite sister. She raised a family of six children, and her home was to provide her eminent brother with opportunities for 'japes' in a large family all over again.

As a graceful, strong young tree
He will live on joyously.

Slender, thoughtful, timid maid
Like a young fawn in the shade.

Frederick Joseph (1859-1866), with Edward (right). 'Joe' was Edward's inseparable companion through early childhood. Lucy remembered:

He was called the 'Beethoven' of the family, having very remarkable aptitude for music from the time he could sit up in his chair, but he was not strong and a source of great anxiety to his parents, and after much suffering he passed away in the dawn of a September day in the seventh year of his age.

Francis Thomas (1861-1928). 'Frank' also had musical ability, but he lacked Edward's nervous energy. He married, succeeded to the family business, and lived an uneventful life in Worcester as a local musician, much as his father had done before him.

Helen Agnes (1864-1939). 'Dot' fulfilled the traditional duties of the youngest daughter by remaining at home to look after her parents. Later she became a nun, and ultimately rose to be Mother General of the Dominicans in England.

The bank of the Severn across from the old
Water-works, Worcester.

*I am still at heart the dreamy child who used to be
found in the reeds by Severn side with a sheet of
paper trying to fix the sounds and longing for
something very great. I am still looking for this . . .*

SIR EDWARD ELGAR · 1921

In 1869 the Elgar children conceived an elaborate
dramatic production. Edward took charge of the music,
and they all worked on it for more than two years:

*By means of a stage-allegory . . .it was proposed to
show that children were not properly understood.
The scene was a 'Woodland Glade', intersected by a
brook; the hither side of this was our fairyland;
beyond, small and distant, was the ordinary life which
we forgot as often as possible. The characters, on
crossing the stream, entered fairyland and were
transfigured.*

*Our orchestral means were meagre: a pianoforte,
two or three strings, a flute and some improvised
percussion were all we could depend upon; the double-
bass was of our own manufacture and three pounds
of nails went into its making . . . But we had the
gorgeous imagination of youth, and the ubiquitous
piano became a whole battery of percussion, a whole
choir of brass or an array of celestial harps as
demanded by the occasion.*

Nevertheless the music Edward wrote for the play
had to be intensely practical. At one point, for example:

*. . . the bass consist[ed] wholly of three notes
(A, D, G) the open strings of the (old English) double-
bass. The usual player [myself] was wanted for stage
management, but the simplicity of the bass made it
possible for a child who knew nothing of music on
any instrument to grind out the bass.*

Nervous, sensitive & kind
Displays no vulgar frame of mind.

ANNE ELGAR on 'Ed'

. . . a most miserable-looking lad — legs like
drumsticks — nothing of a boy about him.
One great characteristic, always doing
something. When he stopped away from
school, which he did about a third of the time,
it was not merely to play truant.

HUBERT LEICESTER

In studying scores the first which came into
my hands were the Beethoven symphonies . . .
they were difficult for a boy to get in
Worcester . . . I, however, managed to get
two or three, and I remember distinctly the
day I was able to buy the Pastoral Symphony.
I stuffed my pockets with bread and cheese
and went out into the fields to study it. That
was what I always did.

Claines Churchyard, in the countryside to the
north of the city. Here Edward often went to
study a new score, sitting amongst the
gravestones of his grandparents.

When I resolved to become a musician and found that the exigencies of life would prevent me from getting any tuition, the only thing to do was to teach myself . . .

. . . I am self-taught in the matter of harmony, counter-point, form, and, in short, the whole of the 'mystery' of music . . First was Catel, and that was followed by Cherubini. The first real sort of friendly leading I had, however, was from 'Mozart's Thorough-bass School'. There was something in that to go upon — something human.

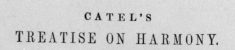

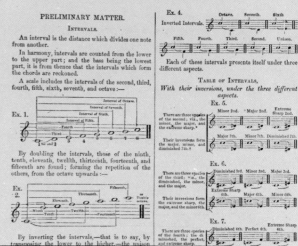

I told my mother once when I was young that I wouldn't be content until I received a letter from abroad addressed to

Edward Elgar, England.

I attended as many of the Cathedral services as I could . . . The putting of the fine new organ into the Cathedral at Worcester was a great event, and brought many organists to play there at various times. I went to hear them all. The services at the Cathedral were over later on Sunday than those at the Catholic church, and as soon as the voluntary was finished at the church I used to rush over to the Cathedral to hear the concluding voluntary.

1872 July 14 Ted played the organ at church for Mass first time.

Diary of LUCY ELGAR

As time went on he took over more and more of his father's duties at St. George's, which included writing some music for the choir.

Five of us established a wind quintet. We had two flutes, an oboe, a clarionet, and a bassoon, which last I played . . . There was no music at all to suit our peculiar requirements . . . so I used to write the music.

We met on Sunday afternoons, and it was an understood thing that we should have a new piece every week. The sermons in our church used to take at least half an hour, and I spent the time composing the thing for the afternoon.

The wind quintet: Frank Exton and Frank Elgar (seated); William Leicester, Edward Elgar, Hubert Leicester.

In 1877, when he was twenty, Edward briefly visited London. There he discovered the orchestral concerts at the Crystal Palace:

. . . many new works were produced and compositions of established repute were played, which I wanted to know.

He began going up to London for a day at a time whenever he could scrape together the railway fare.

. . . he always spoke almost reverentially of [the concerts] which August Manns conducted at the Crystal Palace. I think it was the attendance at those concerts . . . that fired his ambition and turned the scales on the side of serious composition.

W. H. REED

[In 1878] I . . . ruled a score for the same instruments and with the same number of bars as Mozart's G Minor Symphony, and in that framework I wrote a symphony, following as far as possible the same outline in the themes and the same modulation. I did this on my own initiative, as I was groping in the dark after light, but looking back after thirty years I don't know any discipline from which I learned so much.

EDWARD ELGAR   1904

16

From the moment he had first picked up a violin at the age of twelve, Edward had no doubt of having found his instrument. After some lessons with a friend of his father's he had found his way into several local musical groups:

Then I began to teach on my own account, and spent such leisure as I had in writing music. It was music of a sort — bad, very bad . . .

OVERTURE.

SONG........

THE BAND.

1st Violins.		Double Basses.
Mr. E. W. Elgar, *Principal.*	Mr. Dyson.	Mr. Brookes.
Mr. Rooney.	Mr. Grove.	Mr. Hopkins.
Mr. d'Egville.	Mr. Brookes.	Mr. Tyler.
Mr. Weaver.	Mr. Brewer.	*Flutes.*
Mr. Pountney.	*Violas.*	Mr. Hadley.
Mr. Hadley, jun.	Mr. Elgar.	Mr. Graves.
Mr. Whitehead.	Mr. Mather.	*Clarinets.*
Mr. Quarterman.	Mr. Smith.	Mr. Griffiths.
2nd Violins.		Mr. Whinfield.
Mr. W. H. Elgar.	*Violoncellos.*	*Oboe.*
Mr. Hopkins.	Mr. Meredith.	Mr. F. Elgar.
Mr. Bammert.	Mr. Surman.	*Drums.*
Mr. Charke.	Dr. Woodward.	Mr. C. Jones.
Mr. Wall.	Mr. Shepherd.	*Cymbals.*
Mr. Jones.	Mr. George.	Mr. H. J. Hadley.
	Mr. Corkran.	

Solo Violin .. .. Mr. EDWARD ELGAR.

Conductor .. .. MR. ALFRED CALDICOTT, Mus. Bac.

In 1879 Edward secured a conducting appointment: he became bandmaster of an Attendants' Orchestra at the County Lunatic Asylum. In addition to a salary of £32 *per annum*, he was to be paid an additional 5s. for each polka or quadrille he might compose for the band. The Asylum was at Powick, on the road between Worcester and Malvern, and he went there one day of every week during the next five years.

AIR DE BALLET FOR ORCHESTRA ......*Edward Elgar.*

(First time of performance).

At the end of his twenties, Edward's musical progress was to be measured by such things as the extension of his teaching practice to the fashionable town of Malvern, eight miles to the south west of Worcester.

Mr. Edward Elgar,

Violinist,

(Pupil of Herr A. Pollitzer, London),

BEGS to announce that he visits Malvern and neighbourhood to give Violin Lessons, advanced and elementary. Also Lessons in Accompaniment and Ensemble playing.

For Terms, &c., address 4, Field Terrace, Worcester.

The round of activities that defined his life as a local musician offered no escape. Attempts to find a place in London came to nothing. When after years of trying he managed to make some headway with a larger orchestral composition, the Birmingham conductor he consulted was discouraging:

I showed it old Stockley & he candidly said he could not read the Score & it sounded to him disconnected. So I have retired into my shell & live in hopes of writing a polka someday — failing that a single chant is probably my fate.

. . . a spare, dark, shy young man . . . looking at me with a gaze that was at once difficult and aloof — a look that I was to see many a time in after years — as if he was half here and half in some other place beyond our ken.

A.B.L-W.

*He took a room in Malvern for teaching and advertised
it in the local paper. This notice reached a certain lady
living in the depths of the country nine miles away
on the borders of Worcestershire and Gloucestershire,
and she decided to have lessons. After the old coachman
had driven her to Malvern for two or three months,
he was heard to say that he thought there was more
in it than music . . .*

CARICE ELGAR BLAKE

Caroline Alice Roberts came to Mr. Elgar's Malvern
studio in October 1886. She was thirty-eight, devoted
to the arts, and the author of two published novels. She
lived with her widowed mother at Hazeldine House,
Redmarley, the home purchased by her late father,
Major-General Sir Henry Roberts, on his retirement from
the Army.

Alice soon brought Mr. Elgar as a
guest to Hazeldine. But in the
following year Lady Roberts died.
Alice's aunts then made clear their
disapproval of her connection with
the young music teacher.

Braving family opposition, Alice announced her engagement to Mr. Elgar in September 1888, and began to receive instruction in the Catholic faith. Both were anxious to cut local ties and pursue the life of their dreams in London. On 8 May 1889 they were married at the Brompton Oratory.

. . . I must tell you how happy I am in my new life & what a dear, loving companion I have & how sweet everything seems & how understand-able *existence seems to have grown . . . I think all the difficult problems are now solved and — well I don't worry myself about 'em now!*

EDWARD ELGAR   6 October 1889

In London the Elgars first occupied furnished rooms. Then they were lent an accommodation by some cousins of Alice's. But in March 1890 they signed a lease for a house of their own at 51, Avonmore Road, West Kensington. A few days later they moved in.

Almost immediately Edward found himself able to get down to serious composition. It was an orchestral Overture evoking the chivalric life depicted in the pages of Froissart. With Alice's constant encouragement throughout the Spring, he was able to complete it by June. It was the first considerable piece of music he had ever finished.

There was little chance for a performance of the *Froissart Overture* in London, but it was accepted for the Three Choirs Festival, to be held in September at Worcester. Edward would conduct his new work. He had already engaged to play in the Festival orchestra, to supplement the Elgars' meagre resources.

The Worcester Festival of 1890 attracted a young musician called Ivor Atkins, who was a few years later to become organist of Worcester Cathedral:

Sinclair pointed Elgar out to me. There he was, fiddling among the first violins, with his fine intellectual face, his heavy moustache, his nervous eyes and his beautiful hands. The Wednesday Evening came. I had no dress clothes with me . . . so I crept up the steps leading to the back of the Orchestra . . . I watched Elgar's shy entry on to the platform. From that moment my eyes did not leave him, and I listened to the Overture, hearing it in the exciting way one hears music when among the players . . . But there was something else I was conscious of — I knew that Elgar was the man for me, I knew that I completely understood his music, and that my heart and soul went with it.

Back in London the glorious moment faded quickly. As Winter drew on, hopes for further composition evaporated in persistent financial worry. Edward's advertisements for London pupils went unanswered. Alice sold some of her jewellery.

. . . the fogs here are terrifying & make me very ill: yesterday all day & today until two o'clock we have been in a sort of yellow darkness. I groped my way to church this morning & returned in an hour's time a weird and blackened thing . . .

Dec. 30. A. thought this the coldest day she ever felt (and cried with the cold).

By the Spring of 1891 the Elgars had to face the fact that Edward's reputation was only a local one. They would have to go back to Worcestershire.

In June 1891 they took a house at Malvern Link — between Malvern and Worcester — and named it 'Forli', after the early Italian painter of angel musicians.

To make ends meet, Edward taught the violin at The Mount School in Malvern.

The violin lessons were unpopular and the girls who took them a dreary little company who sawed away to the general discomfort in distant rooms.

ROSA BURLEY

He was to remain at it for thirteen years:

Teaching was like turning a grindstone with a dislocated shoulder.

He found a sympathetic spirit in the Headmistress, Rosa Burley:

. . . One day after the ensemble practice he lingered on over tea, silent and diffident . . . Suddenly, without knowing quite how it had begun, I found myself listening to an outpouring of misery . . . The one thing he wanted to do in life, the be-all and end-all of his existence, was to write great music . . . And yet, in spite of this urge, in spite of the glorious possibilities which he knew to be almost within his reach, he had come to a standstill and could do nothing.

ROSA BURLEY

When a daughter was born, Edward devised a name from her mother's – Caroline Alice:

. . . Carice is a most wonderfully lovely infant! everyone turns to gaze at her as she 'sweeps by in her chariot' – (i.e. perambulator). She is a sturdy little minx . . . & has never been ill a day since she came!

At Forli, a *Serenade* emerged out of three earlier pieces. Edward wrote on the MS:

Braut [i.e., Alice] helped a great deal to make these little tunes.

There was always the question of putting the title in a language that might have more 'artistic' *cachet*:

I don't like doing it as my own name is so 'peremptorily' English . . . but I can't afford to wait 'till English is the universal language & don't intend to if I could . . . I would try Greek if it would sell!

Golf – call it a game, a sport or what you will, no one can define golf – is the best form of exercise for writing-men, as it involves no risk of accident, is always ready to hand without waiting for a 'side' . . . and it has the inestimable advantage of being seldom worth seeing and rarely worth reading about.

In the Summer of 1892 a friend of Alice's arranged a holiday for the Elgars in Germany. They visited Bayreuth, but spent most of the time in the mountains:

. . . there are large pine forests & it is so lovely to walk about in them. There are no hedges at all but like an open field as far as you can see.

Edward returned home 'fired with songs'. But it took him more than two years to realize the *Scenes from the Bavarian Highlands,* for which Alice wrote the poems.

A cartoon
by Edward

She gave up her life-long ambition to be a writer of note because she was so sure that a genius had been given into her charge, and it was her proud responsibility to keep him from every worry and difficulty as far as possible. It was she who made, with very little money, a home of which he could be proud and to which his friends could be invited; it was she who ruled the bar lines in all his scores and wrote in the choral parts when required, thereby saving him hours of manual labour; it was she who walked nearly two miles in sunshine or pouring rain to post the precious parcels of MSS.

CARICE ELGAR BLAKE

The care of a genius is enough of a life work for any woman.

ALICE ELGAR

In the Summer of 1897 the idea for a new work came from Edward's mother, who was now seventy-five:

. . . we stood at the door looking along the back of the [Malvern] Hills — the Beacon was in full view — I said Oh! Ed. Look at the lovely old Hill. Can't we write some tale about it. I quite long to have something worked up about it; so full of interest and so much historical interest . . . and in less than a month he told me Caractacus was all cut and dried.

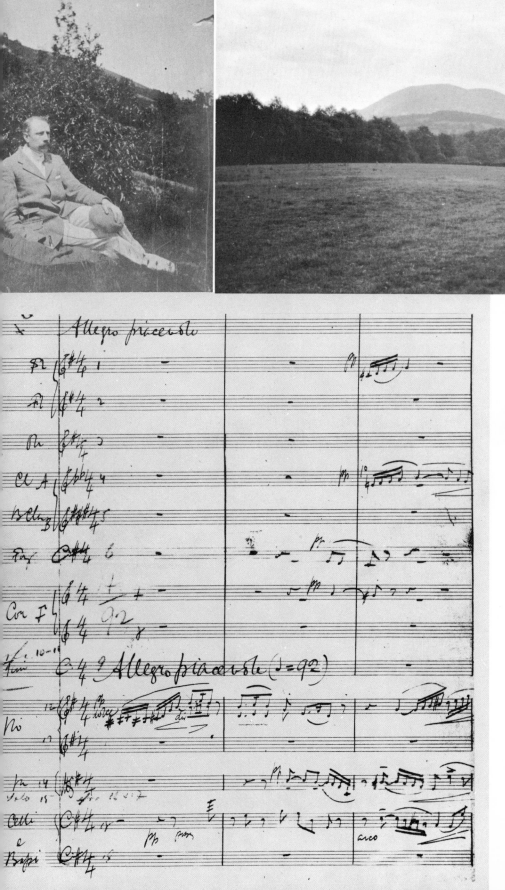

The title-character in the new Cantata was the ancient British general who had defended the Malvern Hills against the invading Romans. No work of Elgar's was ever to have stronger associations with the landscape of his childhood.

Caractacus: A 'Woodland Interlude', evoking a forest near the Severn in early morning.

Anne and William Elgar in old age. In 1902, during the last months of her life, Anne wrote of her son:

. . . what can I say to him the dear one — I feel that he is some great historic person — I cannot claim a little bit of him now he belongs to the big world.

I. 'C.A.E.' – Alice Elgar herself.

II. 'H.D.S-P.' – Hew David Stuart-Powell, a pianist friend.

III. 'R.B.T.' – Richard Baxter Townshend, an eccentric country gentleman.

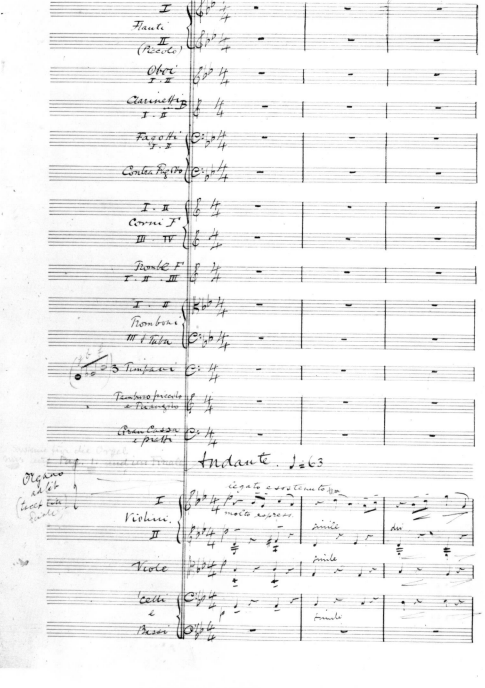

IV. 'W.M.B.' – William Meath Baker, a vigorous squire.

V. 'R.P.A.' – Richard Penrose Arnold, a son of the poet Matthew Arnold.

VI. 'Ysobel' – Isabel Fitton, a viola pupil of E.E.'s.

VII. 'Troyte' – Arthur Troyte Griffith, a Malvern architect.

One evening [*in the Autumn of 1898*] *after a long and tiresome day's teaching, aided by a cigar, I musingly played on the piano the theme as it now stands. The voice of C.A.E. asked with a sound of approval*

 'What is that?'

 I answered 'Nothing — but something might be made of it; Powell would have done this (Variation 2) or Nevinson would have looked at it like this (Variation 12).'

So the *'Enigma' Variations* were born, each identity concealed behind initials or a code:

. . . I've written the variations each one to represent the mood of the 'party' . . . & have written what I think they wd. have written — if they were asses enough to compose.

The première took place on 19 June 1899 in London, under the brilliant conductorship of Hans Richter. The event commanded instant national attention in musical circles. Sir Hubert Parry, for example, was heard to say:

I heard yesterday Richter perform the 'Enigma' Variations by a Mr. Elgar, which is the finest work I have listened to for years. Look out for this man's music; he has something to say and knows how to say it.

XIV. 'E.D.U.' — compounded of Alice's nickname for E.E., a diminutive of the German 'Eduard'.

XIII. '* * *' — Lady Mary Lygon, sister of Lord Beauchamp of Madresfield.

XII. 'B.G.N.' — Basil Nevinson, a 'cellist.

VIII. 'W.N.' — Winifred Norbury, the musical sister in a county family.

IX. 'Nimrod' — A. J. Jaeger of Novellos the publishers, a very close friend.

X. 'Dorabella' — Dora Penny, a girl fascinated by Elgar's genius.

XI. 'G.R.S.' — The initials are those of Dr. Sinclair (left), organist of Hereford Cathedral, but the real subject is his bulldog, Dan.

In March 1899 the Elgars moved to a house in the Wells Road, Malvern. Edward devised a name for their new home out of the family initials C., A., and E. Elgar: 'Craeg Lea'.

'A country life I find absolutely essential to me, and here the conditions are exactly what I require. As you see' (and Dr. Elgar moved over to the large window which takes up the whole of one side of the study) '. . . I get a wonderful view of the surrounding country. I can see across Worcestershire, to Edgehill, the Cathedral of Worcester, the Abbeys of Pershore and Tewkesbury, and even the smoke from round Birmingham.'

Edward with his bicycle 'Mr. Phoebus'.

There cannot have been a lane within twenty miles of Malvern that we did not ultimately find. We cycled to Upton, to Tewkesbury, to Hereford, to the Vale of Evesham, to Birtsmorton . . . to the lovely villages on the west side of the Hills — everywhere.

ROSA BURLEY

Edward with Carice, aged ten, in 1900:

She was a dear little girl, very properly behaved and rather prim, and she did try so hard to keep her father in order!

DORA PENNY

A crucial opportunity came with an invitation to write a major work for
the Birmingham Festival of 1900. After much thoughtful searching among
the books in his library at Craeg Lea, Edward selected Cardinal Newman's
poem *The Dream of Gerontius* as his subject:

*The poem has been soaking in my mind for at least eight years. All that time
I have been gradually assimilating the thoughts of the author into my own
musical promptings.*

The early months of 1900 were entirely devoted to the new work.

As usual with Elgar, the whole composition was first written out in short
score, with the accompaniment mostly on two staves.

The Elgars had taken a remote cottage north of Malvern as a retreat. It was called Birchwood Lodge, and here during the Summer of 1900 Edward finished the full score of *Gerontius*:

. . . the trees are singing my music — or have I sung theirs? . . .It's too lovely here.

3 August 1900: *I cycled over from Ledbury . . . to lunch with him — in those days I seldom went abroad without my camera. On arrival at the cottage I was shown up into Elgar's workroom, where he sat at a huge table absolutely covered with musical MSS. . . . His first words after the usual greetings were to the effect that he was greatly relieved at having that instant written his name under the score of the last bar . . . indeed the ink was not yet dry . . . I begged Elgar to remain just as he was while I went down and fetched my camera . . .*

WILLIAM ELLER

Fine.

"This is the best of me; for the rest, I ate, and drank, and slept, loved and hated, like another; my life was as the vapour, and is not; but this I saw and knew: this, if anything of mine, is worth your memory."

Edward Elgar.

Birchwood Lodge.

August 1900

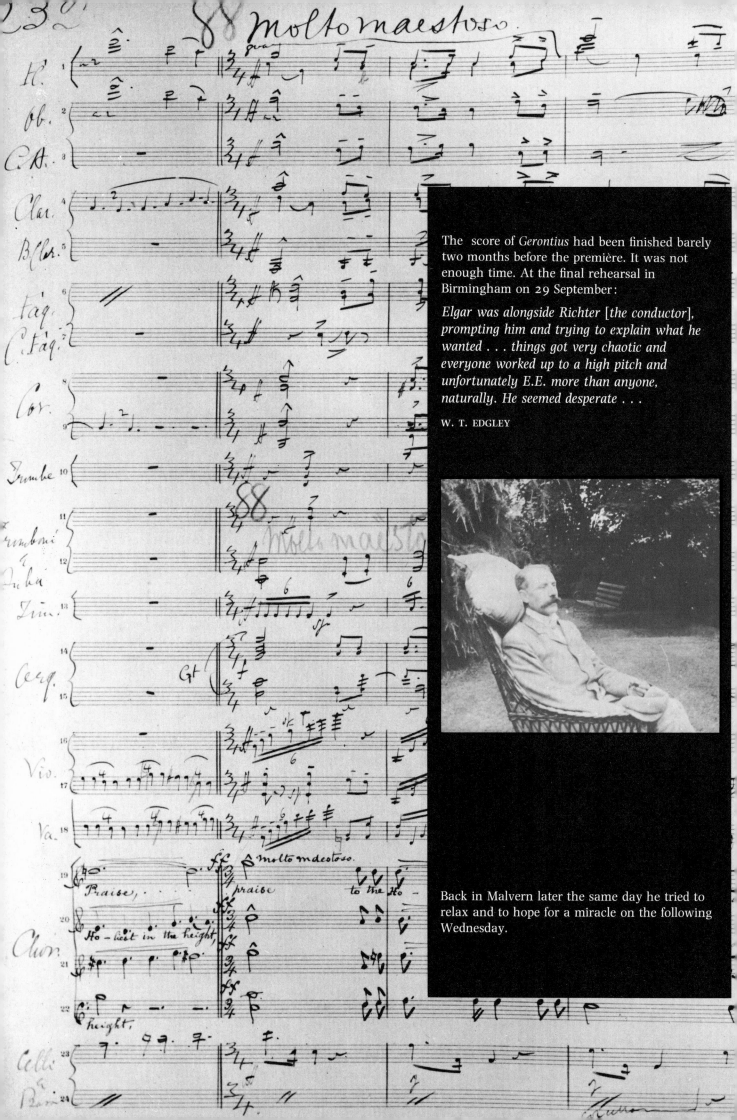

The score of *Gerontius* had been finished barely two months before the première. It was not enough time. At the final rehearsal in Birmingham on 29 September:

Elgar was alongside Richter [the conductor], prompting him and trying to explain what he wanted . . . things got very chaotic and everyone worked up to a high pitch and unfortunately E.E. more than anyone, naturally. He seemed desperate . . .

W. T. EDGLEY

Back in Malvern later the same day he tried to relax and to hope for a miracle on the following Wednesday.

89 Animato

3 October 1900. Soloists more or less inadequate, chorus repeatedly losing pitch and coherent ensemble, the conductor Hans Richter beside himself as the wretched première dragged endlessly on.

On the whole the critics were not unfair in recognizing an important statement behind the badly flawed performance. But Elgar had set too much store by it:

I have worked hard for forty years & at the last, providence denies me a decent hearing of my work: so I submit — I always said God was against art . . . I have allowed my heart to open once — it is now shut against every religious feeling & every soft, gentle impulse for ever.

No more explicit reaction to the whole
Gerontius experience could have been devised
than the musical evocation of London life that
Elgar undertook within three weeks of the
Birmingham Festival:

*Cockaigne was suggested to me one dark day
in the Guildhall: looking at the memorials of
the city's great past & knowing well the history
of its unending charity, I seemed to hear far
away in the dim roof a theme, an echo of some
noble melody . . .*

Progress with *Cockaigne* was interrupted by the
occurrence of a theme of such quality that
Elgar hoped it might become the vehicle for the
Symphony he had always wanted to write.
But nothing came of it. In the depths of the
Winter he returned to the Overture.

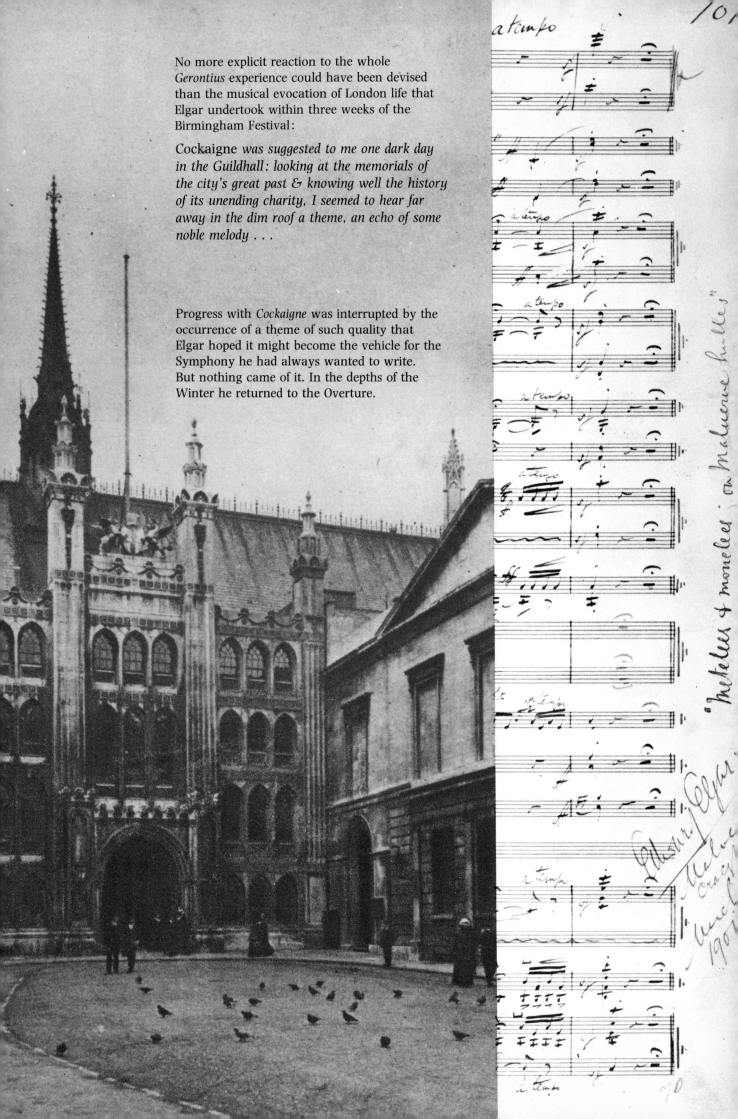

The completion of the new work on 24 March 1901 was marked with a quotation from *Piers Plowman* that contrasted with Ruskin as strongly as *Cockaigne* itself did with *Gerontius*:

Meatless and moneyless on Malvern Hills.

To fulfill the last irony, *Cockaigne*'s première was a huge success.

When Richter conducted a sumptuous performance of *Cockaigne*, Elgar could only write:

. . . it has taught me that I am not satisfied with my music and must do, or rather try to do, something better and nobler.
I hope the Symphony I am trying to write will answer to these higher ideals . . .

Patten Wilson's cover design for *Cockaigne*.

ELGAR.

A drawing by Ernest Forbes.

In May 1901 Elgar showed Dora Penny a new March called *Pomp and Circumstance*:

I've got a tune that will knock 'em — knock 'em flat!

It was almost certainly the melody that had interrupted *Cockaigne* by raising his hope for a Symphony. Now, after many months of frustration, it had been used up in a 'Military March'. Many years later the recollection was still tinged with regret:

A tune like that comes once in a lifetime.

Henry Wood conducted the London première of *Pomp and Circumstance*:

The people simply rose and yelled. I had to play it again — with the same result; in fact, they refused to let me go on with the programme. After considerable delay [and] merely to restore order, I played the march a third time. And that, I may say, was the one and only time in the history of the Promenade concerts that an orchestral item was accorded a double encore.

For the Three Choirs Festival week in September 1901 W. M. Baker organized a house party at Hasfield Court, his home near Gloucester. Among the guests were the Elgars and A. J. Jaeger. Between performances in the Cathedral there was a continuously evolving charade with Baker's sons, arising out of their enthusiasm for Scott's novel *Redgauntlet*. Elgar took the part of the disreputable pirate Nanty Ewart.

We boys were in the garden waiting for Nanty to come out. He had waved to us from his bedroom window so I went indoors to meet him. In the hall I saw Mrs. Elgar, a packet of letters in her hand, the afternoon post having just come. She was going to take them upstairs but as she saw Nanty coming down, she waited and held the letters out to him.

'But I'm going out now', he said, taking them from her and, with a very Nantyish oath, he threw them down on the floor and they scattered in all directions.

'Oh, Edward, that was naughty!'

I picked the letters up and gave them to her. Remarking quietly 'These must be answered at once', she held them out to him. With a shout of ribald laughter he took them from her and went straight back, upstairs, without another word. I went out and told the boys that Nanty couldn't come just yet. We did not see him until tea time.

A great 'Nanty Ewart' correspondence grew up and flourished during the many months that Elgar waited for a new creative inspiration.

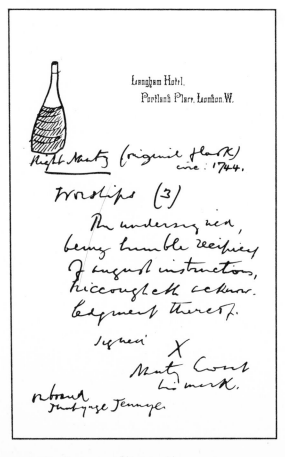

'After the duel' — Elgar, holding a camera, with Jaeger (right) and other members of the Hasfield Court house party in the background.

Dr. Elgar.

It was not until the end of 1901 that *The Dream of Gerontius* was given a successful performance – and then it was not in England but at Düsseldorf.

In May 1902 the Elgars went to Düsseldorf for a second performance of *Gerontius* there. The work and its composer received an enormous acclaim.

A commemorative card.

Garten der Tonhalle.   Gruss. aus Düsseldorf

Alice's postcard sending the news home to Carice.

On the day following the performance there was a luncheon to honour Elgar. Richard Strauss gave the toast:

I drink to the welfare and success of the first English progressivist, Meister Edward Elgar, and of the young progressive school of English composers.

It was the beginning of Elgar's international reputation.

Elgar was asked to compose an Ode for the Coronation of King Edward VII and Queen Alexandra, which was to take place in June 1902. Hearing that the King had liked *Pomp and Circumstance* well enough to suggest that it should be sung, Elgar asked the librettist A. C. Benson to fit words to the great tune. Benson produced a set of verses beginning:

'Land of Hope and Glory . . .'

The music was finished in good time, and Elgar was to conduct the première during Coronation Week in the presence of Their Majesties.

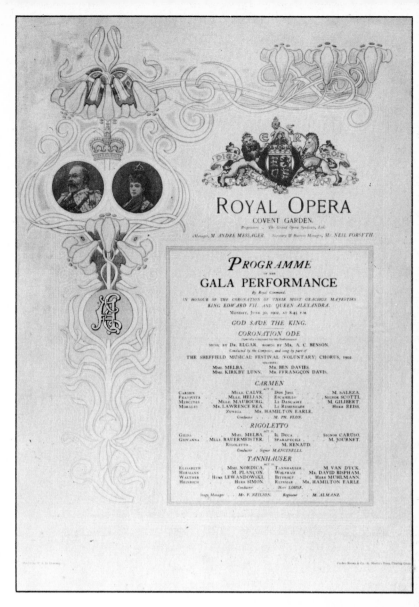

A performance that never took place: the original première of the *Coronation Ode*.

The day before he was to go to London for the performance, Elgar was bicycling with a friend in the country. They stopped at a little roadside pub for tea:

People were already going up to London in great numbers. E. was in a good mood and looking forward to the next day . . .We had just finished tea and were preparing to go when the landlady rushed in saying 'Oh! Sir. The Coronation is put off, the King is ill and is to have an operation at once. The news is just in at the Post Office.'

ROSA BURLEY

Elgar wrote to his friend, Jaeger:

Don't, for heaven's sake, sympathise with me — I don't care a tinker's damn! It gives me three blessed sunny days in my own country (for which I thank God or the Devil) instead of stewing in town . . . I'm deadly sorry for the King — but that's all.

Despite the apparent failure of the *Gerontius* première, Birmingham had asked Elgar to write a new work for the next Festival in 1903. Trying to find his way back to religious expression, he recalled something said to him during childhood by a schoolmaster:

The Apostles were poor men, young men, at the time of their calling; perhaps before the descent of the Holy Ghost not cleverer than some of you here.

It had made such an impression on the boy for whom ambition so outran opportunity that he never forgot it.

Elgar decided that his work on the Apostles must constitute not just a single oratorio but a trilogy. Thus perhaps he would trace for himself the process by which spiritual illumination can be vouchsafed to 'ordinary men'.

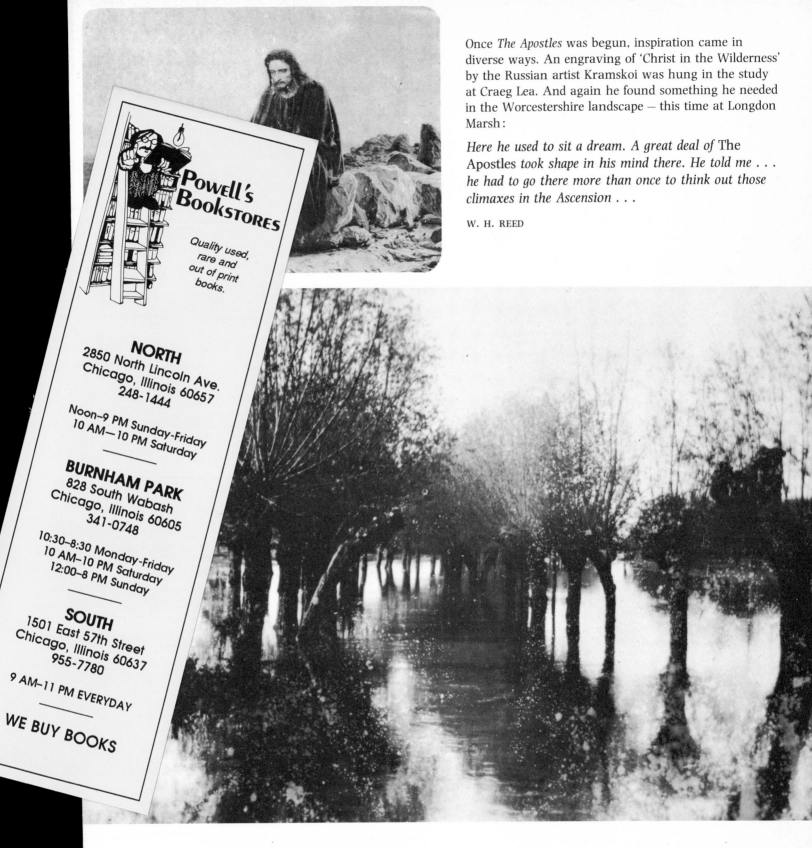

Once *The Apostles* was begun, inspiration came in diverse ways. An engraving of 'Christ in the Wilderness' by the Russian artist Kramskoi was hung in the study at Craeg Lea. And again he found something he needed in the Worcestershire landscape – this time at Longdon Marsh:

Here he used to sit a dream. A great deal of The Apostles *took shape in his mind there. He told me . . . he had to go there more than once to think out those climaxes in the Ascension . . .*

W. H. REED

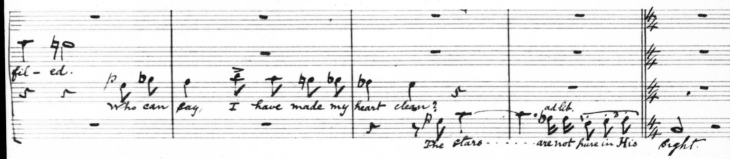

The Apostles made a great success when it was performed at the Birmingham Festival in October 1903. But when would the second and third oratorios appear, and how would so vast a scheme ever be brought to any real conclusion?

43

"THE SKETCH" PHOTOGRAPHIC INTERVIEWS.

"THE VIEW ACROSS MY NATIVE COUNTY IS INSPIRING——"

"——AND, OF COURSE, A PIPE SETTLES MOST DIFFICULTIES,——"

"——BUT THE ACTUAL WRITING IS ALWAYS A TRIAL."

"THE most brilliant champion of the National School of Composition which is beginning to bloom in England." These are the words in which one of the most distinguished German writers on music has summed up the position of Dr. Edward Elgar, whose newest work, "The Apostles," is underlined for production at the Birmingham Musical Festival. So great is the demand for tickets that a second performance is already contemplated during the Festival week. "The Apostles" differs from many other oratorios in that no librettist has been associated with Dr. Elgar in its production. The book has been selected by Dr. Elgar from the words of the Scripture. The subject, he once confided to an interviewer, has thrilled him ever since he was a boy, from which time he regarded the Apostles "from their human side; as men, not as theological figures."

As a boy, the last career which appeared open to him was that of music. True, his father before him was a musician, filling the position of organist at St. George's Catholic Church, Worcester; and in the little village of Broadheath, three miles from that city, his brilliant son was born. When the time came for the choice of a profession, Mr. Elgar senior placed his son in a solicitor's office, with a view to his being articled. Law, however, could not claim the soul which the Muses had marked for their own, and Edward Elgar determined to follow his bent. As a child, he used to sit by his father's side on the stool in the organ-loft, watching him play, and occasionally tried his own hand on the instrument, to his father's great delight.

As an instrumentalist, however, Dr. Elgar, in his youth, decided for the violin, and he took lessons from Herr Pollitzer. But beyond these lessons he has received no musical instruction. All the time he was composing, although he had never received a lesson in instrumentation or counterpoint. That does not say, however, that he was not deeply read in those subjects, for his knowledge was obtained by careful observation, the study of scores, and the practical studies of his own composition.

In those early days of his career there was a Glee Club in Worcester. Dr. Elgar led the small orchestra and accompanied the vocal music, while he also established a wind-quintet, of which he was the fagottist; for it he wrote a great deal of music.

While in Worcester, playing and teaching, Dr. Elgar was a not infrequent visitor to the Saturday Concerts at the Crystal Palace. He would leave home at six o'clock in the morning and not return until late at night in order to hear the orchestral music. At the Crystal Palace, too, several of his earlier works have been performed. It is, however, Dr. Elgar's immovable opinion that his first real introduction to the larger musical public was through the kindness of Mr. W. C. Stockley, the pioneer of orchestral music in the Midlands, to whom Dr. Elgar always expresses sincere and lasting gratitude. Mr. Stockley produced several orchestral works at a time when Dr. Elgar was known only as a violinist. He was, in fact, one of the first-violins in the orchestra in the Town Hall, where his latest work will be produced this month.

When he once had got a hearing, Dr. Elgar's fame soon spread throughout the country, though it was not until the completion of his thirty-sixth Opus that London had the opportunity of forming anything like an adequate judgment of his abilities. This was at a Richter Concert,

"I PLAY OVER THE ORCHESTRAL PARTS (DON'T GO!)——"

"——AND CONSULT MY FRIENDS' PHOTOGRAPHS AS TO THE EFFECT."

"MY REFERENCE LIBRARY IS A CONSTANT SOURCE OF PLEASURE."

LXII.—DR. EDWARD ELGAR.

"THAT'S EDGEHILL—THIRTY MILES AWAY."

"NOTHING LIKE OUTDOOR LIFE. BICYCLING——"

" ——OR A CLIMB—— "

where his "Variations on an Original Theme" for the orchestra was produced by Dr. Richter in June 1899, and created an extraordinary sensation. These "Variations" were character-studies, intended to be portraits of his friends, a description which must seem to the ordinary individual as decidedly fantastic. Musicians saw in them, however, exactly what the composer intended, and they marvelled now at the extraordinary ease and originality of his method, now at his great mastery of contrapuntal knowledge, now at his great manipulation of orchestral effects.

The next year, at the Birmingham Festival, the "Dream of Gerontius" was produced, a work which Dr. Lessmann, perhaps the most celebrated German critic, singled out for special commendation, remarking particularly on the extraordinary independence of its outlook; while Dr. Julius Buths, the famous conductor of Düsseldorf, was so enchanted with it that he determined to produce it in Germany, and to that end himself translated the libretto. The success of this performance was so great that the "Dream" was repeated at the Lower Rhine Festival—a unique event in the annals of British music. Since then it has been given many times in Germany, and is underlined for production on several occasions between now and Christmas in various cities in the Fatherland, while during the same interval it will be given at least eight times in the United States. These circumstances are so unusual that England may well pride herself on the achievement of one of her sons whose "Gerontius" has been declared to be "the greatest composition of the last hundred years, with the single exception of the Requiem of Brahms."

He is a great admirer of Wagner, in whose footsteps he not unnaturally walks, though there is nothing of the imitator in his method, for it is "always original and always noble," as one of his critics has said.

Personally, with his slight physique, his brown hair, cut short, and his heavy moustache, his quick, nervous movements and quick speech, Dr. Elgar gives no hint of the popular notion of a musician, and might rather pass for an Army officer in mufti than anything else.

Musician, however, he is to the core, and if his intention to write an opera is fulfilled, a great step will be taken towards the advancement of a form of musical composition in which we are beaten by other nations of the world. Dr. Elgar's opera, if it is written, will be of a heroic or fantastic character, for, as he has himself said, "Art has nothing to do with the frivolous, nor have I," a statement which may well be believed in view of what was said of him in November 1900, when the Honorary Degree of Doctor of Music was conferred upon him by the University of Cambridge. Then the orator, after referring to several of his most important works, declared, "If ever this votary of the Muse of Song looked from the hills of his present home at Malvern, from the cradle of English poetry, the scene of the vision of Piers Plowman, and from the British Camp, with its legendary memories of his own 'Caractacus,' and in the light of the rising sun sees the towers of Tewkesbury and Gloucester and Worcester, he might recall in that view the earlier stages of his career, and confess, with modest pride, like the bard in the 'Odyssey'—

Self-taught I sing; 'tis Heaven, and Heaven alone,
Inspires my song with music all its own."

" ——OR GOLF (JUST NINE HOLES), IS WONDERFULLY REFRESHING."

"THIS FOR THE MATCH, I THINK."

"DON'T SULK, LITTLE ONE!"

Success brought friends in high places, and a three-day festival devoted entirely to his music was being planned in London for March 1904. But privately Elgar was unhappy. The continuing creative frustration of the unwritten Symphony especially had begun to tell on his health. In November Alice decided to take him to Italy for the Winter: there perhaps he might find the Symphony at last.

It was Elgar's first sight of Italy. They stayed at Bordighera and Alassio, where E.E. recorded early impressions with his camera: a Roman bridge (with Alice, Carice, and Rosa Burley), a monastery ruin, and the tall 'Roman' pines.

But the weather was dreadful indeed. Bitterly cold rain and wind seemed to pursue them everywhere. Elgar wrote:

. . . one step outside the door & I am cut in two, numbed and speechless: I have never regretted anything more than this horribly disappointing journey . . .

*Alassio. Jan 3 1904 . . . this visit has been, is,
artistically a complete failure & I can do nothing:
we have been perished with cold, rain & gales . . .
The Symphony will not be written in this sunny(?)
land . . . I am trying to finish a Concert overture for
Covent Garden instead of the Sym . . .*

Some progress was made, but when he received an
invitation to dine with the King at Marlborough House
Elgar was glad to cut short the Italian visit at the end of
the month.

Back at Craeg Lea Elgar worked frantically to finish the
Overture in time for the Covent Garden Festival. The
final portion of score went to the publishers less than
three weeks before the scheduled première. Jaeger
characterised the scene in Novello's at the beginning
of March as 'Bedlam':

*. . . try as we will, with every Copyist 'going' —
& being badgered — we can't do more than we are
doing to get this thing finished in time for your
Rehearsal on the 9th.*

Somehow a barely sufficient number of orchestral parts
was got ready, but only by dint of Elgar himself proof-
reading and correcting nearly the whole lot.

The King and Queen attended both the Monday and Tuesday performances. At the final concert on the Wednesday evening, *In the South* was given pride of place immediately following the interval, and Elgar himself conducted the première.
Alice wrote to Edward's sister Polly in Worcestershire:

I wish you cd have seen E in his full dress, he did look so nice . . . his reception when he came to conduct was tremendous & after the Overture & Marches . . . he was presented with a splendid wreath . . . the Queen was there again, & sent for E. & was very charming.

For the Elgars themselves the whole week was filled with parties and receptions:

. . . dear little Mrs. E. . . . must have been in the 7th Heaven of Happiness. Such swells they met, from the Queen downwards.

A. J. JAEGER

At Lord Northampton's house they were introduced to the Prime Minister, Arthur Balfour:

. . . he & E. had much talk.

On 22 June, while E.E. was away at Durham receiving an honorary degree, a letter from the Prime Minister arrived at Craeg Lea. Alice put it in the safe. As soon as Edward walked into the house:

A. told E. of letter, he sd. with such a light in his face 'Has it come?' . . . Then he opened the letter & found H.M. was going to make him a Knight.

Next day Edward cycled over to Stoke to tell his old father. Since the death of his wife in 1902 W. H. Elgar had been living with his daughter Polly and her family. Polly's daughter May photographed the proud, intimate moment.
Edward's youngest sister Dot, now a nun, wrote to him:

How good of you to go & tell Dad — if only dear old Mother could have heard this her joy & pride in 'her boy' would have been complete. I do with all my heart congratulate you both . . .

On 4 July Edward went up to London to try on his court suit, and the next day to Buckingham Palace:

The King smiled charmingly and said 'Very pleased to see you here, Sir Edward.'

The Elgars had decided that they must move from Craeg Lea:

. . . we are almost certainly leaving here on account of the building which will spoil our heavenly view.

Early in 1904 they had seen a large house called 'Plas Gwyn' on the eastern side of Hereford – still close to the Malvern Hills. It would be far more expensive to rent than 'Craeg Lea', but they decided to take it.

The Elgars moved into Plas Gwyn on 1 July 1904. One of their first visitors was Dora Penny. Alice greeted her with:

I think great music can be written here, dear Dora, don't you?

Plas Gwyn in Summer: Edward is on the veranda
outside his study.

Alice at the sundial in the front garden.

To Carice

Dear little ship, go forth
High-hearted, south or north.
   Spread white and wide thy sails
Buoyed with the Hope that never fails.
    Soon dawns the day
  When thou must take thy way;
    Must leave the lea
  And sail upon the sea,
    And breast the tides
  Which lash thy shrinking sides,
    And brave the blasts
  Which rock thy quiv'ring masts.

Heed not the flying years;
Pass on, unvext by fears.
   Steer bravely still, and find
A strange new strength in every wind.
    May fortune pour
  For thee her richest store.
    May joy be thine,
  All love around thee shine.
    Then at life's end,
  We pray that Heaven send
    Thee, God's own peace
The port, where waves and winds shall cease.

C.A.E.

The first sizable work to be written at Plas Gwyn was an *Introduction and Allegro* for strings. It was finished early in 1905.

Some three years ago, in Cardiganshire, I thought of writing a brilliant piece for string orchestra. On the cliff, between blue sea and blue sky, thinking out my theme, there came up to me the sound of singing. The songs were too far away to reach me distinctly, but one point common to all was impressed upon me, and led me to think, perhaps wrongly, that it was a real Welsh idiom — I mean the fall of a third . . . Fitting the need of the moment I made the tune which appears in the Introduction and in the coda of this work; and so my gaudery became touched with romance . . .

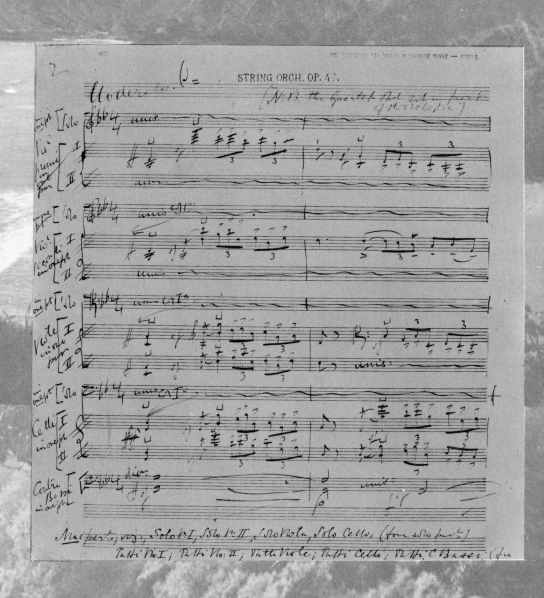

The sketch was forgotten until a short time ago, when it was brought to my mind by hearing, far down our own Valley of the Wye, a song similar to those so pleasantly heard on Ynys Lochtyn . . . This I have now completed and, although there may be (and I hope there is) a Welsh feeling in the one theme — . . . 'All the waters in Wye cannot wash the Welsh blood out of its body' — the work is really a tribute to that sweet borderland where I have made my home.

How and when do I do my music? I can tell you very easily. I come into my study at nine o'clock in the morning and I work till a quarter to one. I don't do any inventing then, for that comes anywhere and everywhere . . . The morning is devoted to revising and orchestration . . .

The composer wrote at a table in the centre of the room . . . At Plas Gwyn, in a much larger study, Elgar used a small mahogany dinner-table as his writing-table . . . This plan made room for all sorts of accessories: letter basket, ink-pots and tray, stationery cabinet, &c., with plenty of room for parcels of proof-sheets, music paper, and books . . .

I once watched him orchestrating something, the 24-stave music paper held at the bottom by his left hand, the first finger at a bar on the lowest line, the right hand and pen running up to the top to do a passage for the flutes, coming down to put in something for the brass, lower for the harp, and below, a whole cascade of notes for the violins.

DORA PENNY

The piano was used only at the end, to try over a section of completed composition:

There is one point Sir Edward makes . . . Music to him was never the keyboard . . . He never evolved his musical thoughts in a keyboard shape, as the early training of so many composers impels them to do. His thoughts came to him, and still do, as abstractions — just music, but clothed in one colour or another, determining their disposition on one line or another of the orchestral score.

Interview with PERCY SCHOLES

In September 1905 Worcester honoured Elgar with the Freedom of the City. The Mayor was his boyhood friend Hubert Leicester, and the ceremony took place in the Guildhall – only a little way down the High Street from the Elgar Music Shop. There in his old rooms above the shop sat W. H. Elgar, too feeble to attend the ceremony but able to watch through the window the procession honouring his son.

12 September 1905: Elgar (wearing the robes of the Yale University doctorate recently conferred) leaves the Worcester Guildhall with Hubert Leicester after the ceremony. It is the Tuesday of Three Choirs Festival week, and the performance of *The Dream of Gerontius* will commence as soon as the civic procession reaches the Cathedral:

[I] *well remember . . . seeing the procession making its way from the Guildhall to the Cathedral with the Mayor, the High Sheriff and all the Aldermen in their civic robes and Elgar walking solemnly in their midst . . . Elgar turned as he passed a certain house in the High Street . . . and saluted an old gentleman whose face could just be seen looking out of an upper window.*

W. H. REED

Every success continued to be clouded by the
thought of the unwritten Symphony. The offer
of a professorship in the new University of
Birmingham promised an alternative mode of
expression that seemed momentarily attractive.
During 1905 and 1906 Elgar delivered eight
lectures.

University of Birmingham.

Inaugural Lecture by the "Richard Peyton"
Professor of Music.

By invitation of the Principal and Senate, PROFESSOR SIR EDWARD ELGAR
has consented to give a FREE PUBLIC LECTURE on

A Future for English Music;

and the date fixed is *Thursday, March 16th*, at 5.45 p.m.   The *Large Lecture
Theatre* of the Midland Institute has been kindly placed at the disposal of the
University for the purpose by the authorities of the Institute, and the attendance
of all students and friends of the University is invited.

Members of the Staff and Undergraduates will wear ordinary academicals.
Students are requested to sit near the front, and Members of the Staff on the Platform.
It is not proposed to issue tickets of admission, but places will be reserved for any member of the Council
and his friends who will kindly send word beforehand to the Secretary of the University.

Elgar felt it his duty to express frankly his own artistic beliefs:

*I hold that the Symphony without a programme is the highest
development of art . . . Perhaps the form is somewhat battered by
the ill-usage of some of its admirers . . . but when the looked-for genius
comes, it may be absolutely revived.*

Elgar's lectures drew immense interest, but again and again his honesty
exceeded his tact. The newspapers made much of it all by publishing
provocative quotations after each lecture, until Elgar wrote to a friend:

I am killed with the University.

He held the professorship for three years, and then thankfully resigned.

During the Autumn of 1905 Elgar commenced serious work on the second oratorio of his 'Apostles' trilogy, which had been promised for the Birmingham Festival the following year. At the end of November Dora Penny came to Plas Gwyn for a visit. She was met in the hall by Alice with a finger on her lips:

'He's hard at work on The Kingdom *— he's been in the study all this morning and he only had a mouthful of luncheon! I've heard wonderful strains every now and then . . .'*

Dinner was just coming in . . . when the study door opened and E.E. appeared.

'Where's dinner?' he said rather roughly . . . He looked up and saw me on the stairs: 'Hullo, you here? I'm busy.' . . .

We went in and had our dinner. He never spoke. When he was not looking at his plate he looked straight in front of him with a rather tense expression. He was very pale and looked tired and drawn. Half-way through dessert he pushed his chair back, hit my hand, which happened to be on the table, quite sharply, and left the room. He banged the study door and turned the key . . .

'He always locks himself in now that the study is downstairs . . . he feels safer!' . . .

So we went back to our drawing-room fire . . . We sat on, talking, reading, working, and when 10.30 came the Lady said:

'Oughtn't you to go to bed, dear Dora? I'm sure you're tired.'

But I said please mightn't I stay up with her, I should so much like to . . . Presently she said:

'Don't you think it would be nice to make ourselves some tea?'
I went with her to the kitchen, and there was a tea-tray all put ready and a large plate of sandwiches covered over, and plates of cake and biscuits. 'It isn't the first time this has happened,' I thought, and carried the tray of eatables into the drawing-room. We had two sandwiches each and took all the rest to the tray on the oak chest [outside the study door].

While we were drinking our tea we heard the piano at last! The piano in the study was an upright and it stood against the wall with its back to the drawing-room fire-place, and the sound seemed to come down the chimney . . . The house was all quiet . . . and we just sat and listened . . . hearing the scene as it grew, phrase by phrase: once a reminder of something in The Apostles *— the Lady and I looked at one another — and then it was all new again.*

I don't know how long he went on playing, but silence came at length and we both realised that it must be very late and that we were greatly in need of another brew of tea. I went out and made it this time, and the hall clock struck half-past one as I passed it. He was playing again when I came back with the tray, but we had not finished a first cup when the music stopped. We heard his key turn, and the Lady got up and opened the drawing-room door.

'Hullo! You still up? and Dorabella too? and tea! Oh, my giddy aunt! This is good!'

. . . After we had drunk up all the tea and eaten all the sandwiches and most of the cake and biscuits we went into the study . . . Then he played the whole of that evening's work, and more, straight through, and we recognised passages we had heard down the chimney. I saw the words,

'The sun goeth down; Thou makest darkness, and it is night . . .' DORA PENN

The Kingdom made an immense impression at Birmingham on 7 October 1906. Such work as this, it was said, would create a wide and enthusiastic public for oratorio in the twentieth century.
But the writing of The Kingdom had taken a psychological toll that was very heavy: as he conducted the première Elgar was observed several times to be weeping. Eighteen months later he told Jaeger that the trilogy would never be completed.

Elgar in his study
at Plas Gwyn,
with his sketches
for *The Kingdom*.

. . . I have been 'Symphony-writing' for years!

That persistent desire had probably contributed to the troubles that beset the composition of *The Kingdom*. For many months after the oratorio's première, however, Elgar's creative life was nearly blank. In June 1907

E. playing great beautiful tune.

It seemed a beginning, but again nothing followed. In November the Elgars went to Rome.

Here is my Mecca & I love it all — note the fact that I am a Pagan not Xtian at present . . . Yes: I am trying to write music . . .

In Rome at last he was able to bring a First Movement out of the 'great beautiful tune'. Then there was part of a Scherzo.

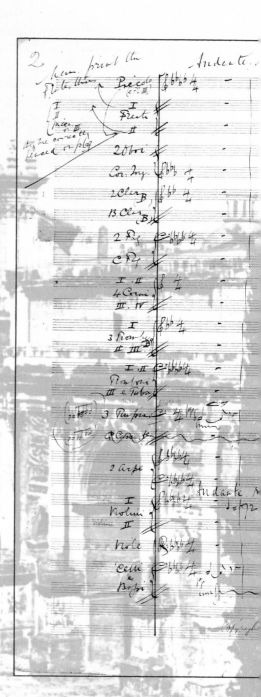

I.

Bowered on sloping hillsides rise
   In sunny glow, the purpling vine:
Beneath the greyer English skies,
   In fair array, the red–gold apples shine.

     To you in snow,
      To us in sun,
       Love is but one;
     Hearts beat and glow
      By oak or vine,
       Friends, always mine.

II.

On and on old Tiber speeds
   Dark with its weight of ancient crime:
Far north, through green and quiet meads,
   Flows on the Wye midst mist and silvering rime.

III.

The pifferari come from far,
   They seek the shrines, and hymn the peace
Which herald angels, 'neath the star,
   Foretold to shepherds, bidding strife to cease.

IV,

Our England sleeps in shroud of snow,
   Bells, sadly sweet, recall life's flight,
And tears, unbid, are wont to flow,
   As 'Noel! Noel!' sounds across the night.

     To you in snow,
      To us in sun,
       Love is but one;
     Hearts beat and glow
      By oak or vine,
       Friends, always mine,

        C. ALICE ELGAR.
          Roma, Dic. 1907.

(For E's music).

The fragile mood of the Elgar household at the end of 1907 is reflected in Alice's 'Christmas Greeting', which they sent as a holiday card that year. Edward set the poem to music, but during their remaining five months in Rome there was little further progress with the Symphony.

Not until he was back at Plas Gwyn did the Symphony begin to move forward again:

June 13 1908 ... I can't answer your letter at this moment. I can't say I have anything more important to do but it must be done & done now. Oh! such a tune.
July 15 ... I am trying to work & am covering sheets of paper to no good end.
July 19 ... Do come over: I am writing heavenly music(!) & it will do you good to hear it ...

So it went on throughout the Summer. At the end of September the Symphony stood finished. It was Elgar's first really big piece of entirely abstract music:

There is no programme beyond a wide experience of human life with a great charity (love) and a massive hope in the future.

Hans Richter (seated), with Elgar and G. R. Sinclair (left). Elgar dedicated the Symphony to Richter —

True Artist and True Friend.

Hans Richter conducted the first performances in Manchester and London. Jaeger attended the London première:

I never in all my experience saw the like. The Hall was packed; any amount of musicians. I saw Parry, Stanford, E. German, J. Corder, E. Faning, P. Pitt, E. Kreuz, etc. The atmosphere was electric ...

After the first movement E.E. was called out; again, several times, after the third, and then came the great moment. After that superb Coda (Finale) the audience seemed to rise at E. when he appeared. I never heard such frantic applause after any novelty nor such shouting ... People stood up and even on their seats to get a view.

E.E. in 'The Ark', Plas Gwyn:

Here Elgar would retire and ease the burden of his destiny as a composer by pretending to be a chemist.

Though he once patented a process for making sulphuretted hydrogen, the legends of his chemical misadventures are legion:

. . . he had made a phosphoric concoction which, when dry, would 'go off' by spontaneous combustion. The amusement was to smear it on a piece of blotting paper and then wait breathlessly for the catastrophe. One day he made too much paste; and, when his music called him and he wanted to go back to the house, he clapped the whole of it into a galli-pot, covered it up, and dumped it into the water-butt, thinking it would be safe there.

Just as he was getting on famously, writing in horn and trumpet parts, and mapping out wood-wind, a sudden and unexpected crash, as of all the percussion
in all the orchestras on earth, shook the room, followed by the 'rushing mighty sound' he had already anticipated in The Kingdom. *The water-butt had blown up: the hoops were rent: the staves flew in all directions; and the liberated water went down the drive in a solid wall.*

Silence reigned for a few seconds. Then all the dogs in Herefordshire gave tongue; and all the doors and windows opened. After a moment's thought, Edward lit his pipe and strolled down to the gate, andante tranquillo, *as if nothing had happened and the ruined water-butt and the demolished flower-beds were pre-historic features of the landscape. A neighbour, peeping out of his gate, called out, 'Did you hear that noise, sir: it sounded like an explosion?' 'Yes', said Sir Edward, 'I heard it: what was it?' The neighbour shook his head; and the incident was closed.*

W. H. REED

Elgar had been thinking of a Violin Concerto for twenty years. Fritz Kreisler had asked him repeatedly for it. During 1909 he made many sketches, but they did not coalesce. Work was interrupted in March 1910 when the Elgars took a flat in London to try the experiment of living in the great city. Edward was apprehensive:

. . . there is really no place for me here . . .

W. H. Reed, a violinist from the London Symphony Orchestra, recalled:

. . . meeting [Elgar], one day in Regent Street, he stopped me to know whether I had any spare time, and if so could I come up to see him . . . He was sketching out something for the fiddle, and wanted to settle, in his own mind, some question of bowing and certain intricacies in the passage-work . . .

When I arrived I found E. striding about with a lot of loose sheets of music paper, arranging them in different parts of the room. Some were already pinned on the backs of chairs, or stuck up on the mantelpiece ready for me to play . . . What we played was a sketchy version of the Violin Concerto. He had got the main

ideas written out, and, as he put it, 'japed them up' to make a coherent piece . . . It was wonderful to note the speed at which he scribbled out another passage or made an alteration or scrapped a sketch altogether as being redundant . . . but soon the parts took shape and were knit together to become an integral part of the Concerto.

The completion of the Violin Concerto in August 1910 brought Elgar deep satisfaction:

. . . it's good! awfully emotional! too emotional but I love it . . . these are times for composition.

He dedicated it to Fritz Kreisler, who was to play the first performance.

Elgar in Queen's Hall rehearsing the Philharmonic Orchestra for the premiére of the Violin Concerto.

10 November 1910: . . . Queen's Hall . . . was simply packed. Kreisler came on looking as white as a sheet . . . but he played superbly. E.E. was also, obviously, very much strung up; but all went well and the ovation at the end was tremendous. Kreisler and E.E. shook hands for quite a long while . . . Finally they came in arm-in-arm.

DORA PENNY

During April 1911 Elgar toured Canada and the American Mid-West to conduct his works for the Sheffield Choir.

A railway platform in the Mid-Western United States: Sir Edward Elgar (left) and the principals of the Sheffield Choir World Tour. In America Elgar felt

every nerve shattered by some angularity, vulgarity, and general horror . . . I loathe & detest every minute of my life here . . . All I can do is to count the days . . .

E.E. at the home of his friend Frank Schuster (to whom he had dedicated *In the South*) near Maidenhead. Schuster stands behind Elgar; at the right is Lord Northampton.

It was a sweet riverside house . . . only a stone's throw from the Thames . . . if Sir Edward wanted to go out in the air . . . we went off together, strolling about the river-bank, watching the small fish in the water and enjoying the quiet beauty of the place.

W. H. REED

While the Violin Concerto was in progress, ideas for a second Symphony were born. The Concerto's première was hardly over before Elgar found himself deeply involved in the new work. It went forward with such speed that before the end of January 1911 the first movement was finished:

I have worked at fever heat and the thing is tremendous in energy.

By the end of February the entire work was before him.

At the end of the score was inscribed 'Venice-Tintagel (1910-11)', suggesting the importance of these recently visited places in the inspiration of the Second Symphony. But between the conception and its execution, King Edward had died. That event determined the work's dedication, and also perhaps the placement of an elegiac *Larghetto* in the central position. Over the entire work went a quotation from Shelley:

'Rarely, rarely comest thou,
Spirit of Delight.'

At the first performance on 24 May 1911, the Second Symphony's heavily charged atmosphere of retrospection emerged as curiously at odds with the bustle of preparation for the new Coronation. For the first time in years a major Elgar premiere failed to hit the mark. Amid the polite applause Elgar, who had conducted, turned to the orchestra leader and whispered:

What is the matter with them, Billy? They sit there like a lot of stuffed pigs.

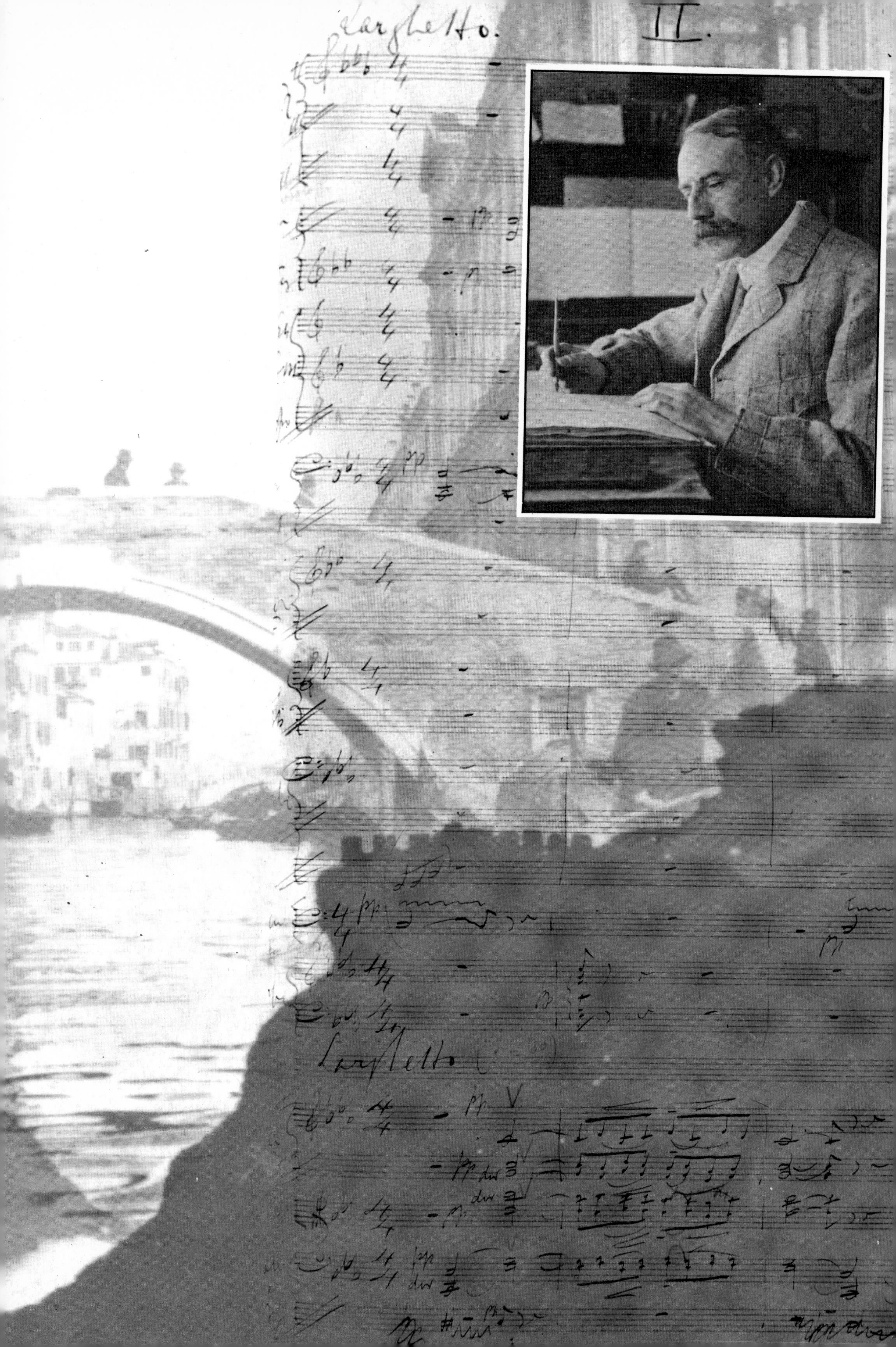
Larghetto.
II.
Larghetto

In the Coronation Honours of 1911 Elgar was given the Order of Merit. Sir Hubert Parry spoke for the whole musical profession when he said to a colleague:

He is the right person for it. You see, he has reached the hearts of the people.

But for the boy who had told his mother he wouldn't be content until he received a letter addressed 'Edward Elgar, England', it seemed to mark an ending:

There's now nothing left for me to achieve.

Self-consciousness about the new Honour emerged in a parody programme Elgar wrote for the Worcester Festival that year. On the day of the Opening Service, the *Side Shows* broadside was almost as ubiquitous as the official Programme itself.

Queer Hardie —
Kier Hardie was one of the earliest Labour M.P.'s. Elgar was a life-long Conservative.

Beecham Guinea Orchestra —
Thomas Beecham was aided in establishing himself as an orchestral conductor by a family fortune made from the famous pills 'worth a guinea a box'.

Mrs. Worthington—
An American friend of the Elgars who regularly attended the Three Choirs Festivals.

Dr. Elizabeth Pastoral —
In the 1911 Festival programme were *Five Elizabethan Pastorals* by Herbert Brewer.

Early Perp. Experts —
Worcester Cathedral had suffered heavily in the puristic 'restorations' of the later nineteenth century.

Miss Grafton —
E.E.'s niece May, who had accompanied the Elgars to Italy.

The Bishop's Residence —
The official residence of the Bishop of Worcester has long been the rather remote Hartlebury Castle.

Bear Pit in College Yard —
The north lawn of the Cathedral was at that moment the scene of archaeological excavation.

WORCESTER FESTIVAL, 1911.

SIDE SHOWS

(By permission of Mr. Queer Hardie, M.P., and in Contemptuous Defiance of the Dean and Chapter).

Monday, 12th September, LECTURE in the Commandery by the O.M., entitled:
" Dyspeptic Hagiology Biologically Considered and Quantitatively Analysed."
Lie-m-Light Illustrations.
" Advertising Quartets" by the Beecham Guinea Orchestra of Coloured Specialists and the Holloway Knockabouts.

Tuesday, 13th September. Popular Day.
BURNING OF HERETICS
(Supply not guaranteed; every endeavour will be made to procure fresh imitations).
FREQUENT PARACHUTE DESCENTS
from the Cathedral Tower by Mrs. Worthington and the Trombones of the Orchestra.
SUMMER SPORTS in the Close (conducted by Dr. Elizabeth Pastoral).
STRIKE MEETING of Composers for a Four-hours' Day and a British Pitch.
MOONLIGHT ASSAULT on the Elgar Tower by the Blacklegs of the Close.
Thereafter minions will raise " L " to the E(d)gar Statue.

Wednesday, 13th September.
GREAT ARSON ACT.
Firing of a Nunnery previously selected by a Committee of blinded Early Perp. Experts. The O.M. will fire the first faggot at Curfew.

Thursday, 14th September.
MIRACULOUS INTERLUDE
Miss Grafton (from Italy, where she has been studying the Science) will sail in a stone coffin (courteously provided by Canon Wilson, who will later on perish at the stake) from the Bridge to the Ferry. *En route* she will jerk a miracle selected by the Commissary of Oaths from a richly-assorted and old-landed parcel. The O.M., dibbling from the stern of the cist with a pig-tailed worm will repeatedly hook poly-carp, laughing daces, and gold-ring-containing perch, thereby administering a considerable slosh in the jaw to St. Mungo, who is expected to be present and make a few remarks for publication (or otherwise).

Friday, 15th September.
GRAND CONCLUDING ECCLESIASTICAL SCENA.
The Bishop of the Diocese, seizing the opportunity to procure a residence in the City, will (preceded by his Examining Chaplain) enter a newly-excavated Bear Pit in College Yard. Buns will be retailed by the Dean and Members of the Chapter at an easy rate.

CONCLUDING FIREWORK DISPLAY by the Minor Canons, Composers, and Prophets.

LEICESTER, TYP., WORCESTER

Ever since their marriage Alice had longed to see her genius appropriately housed in London. By 1911 the constant demands for his presence there had added a consideration that seemed to tip the balance. When they were offered an imposing Hampstead residence designed by Norman Shaw, it appeared as the fulfilment of many dreams. As they were packing up in Hereford, Edward wrote:

I ape royal state, under my wife's kindly direction . . .

The Music Room at Severn House. Music composed here was scored at the large circular table.

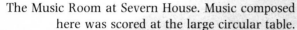

He wistfully named it Severn House, and the Elgars moved in at the beginning of 1912. But when Dora Penny came and remarked that he must be in clover here, E.E. replied:

I don't know about the clover — I've left that behind at Hereford . . .

E.E. in the garden of Severn House with Anthony Goetz, the son of the contralto Muriel Foster.

Hair now very grey, but otherwise unchanged in appearances. Eyes open and shut rapidly and continuously, hands small, slender and nervous . . . Complexion rather dark, almost olive-colour, strong, well-shaped moustache, nose almost hooked. Teeth large, strong, white and show when he smiles. Speaks rapidly, sharply and distinctly. Not very loud but clear.

PHILIP LEICESTER

. . . my wife is a wonderful woman. I play phrases and tunes to her because she always likes to see what progress I have been making. Well, she nods her head and says nothing, or just 'Oh, Edward!' – but I know whether she approves or not, and I always feel that there is something wrong with it if she doesn't.

. . . an indefatigable hostess and marvellous *manager . . .*

FRANK SCHUSTER

Early in 1912 Elgar was asked to write music for *The Crown of India*, an 'Imperial Masque' to celebrate the Indian Coronation of King George V and Queen Mary. The music was largely 'cooked up' from discarded sketches. It proved a great success, and Sir Edward himself conducted the entire run at the Coliseum Theatre.

When I write a big serious work e.g. Gerontius we have had to starve and go without fires for twelve months as a reward: this small effort allows me to buy scientific works I have yearned for and I spend my time between the Coliseum and the old bookshops . . .

The first large work written at Severn House was again a fulfilment of a project long considered – a choral setting of Arthur O'Shaughnessy's *The Music Makers*. Elgar found in the Ode an invitation to evoke

. . . moods which the creative artists suffers . . . for even the highest ecstacy of 'making' is mixed with the consciousness . . . of the artist's responsibility.

The Music Makers was finished on 19 June 1912:

Yesterday was the most awful *day which inevitably occurs when I have completed a work: it has always been so: but this time I promised myself 'a day!' – I should be crowned – it wd be lovely weather – I should have open air & sympathy & everything to mark the end of the work – to get away from the labour part & dream over it happily . . . But – I sent the last page to the printer. Alice & Carice were away for the day & I wandered alone on [Hampstead] Heath – it was bitterly cold – I wrapped myself in a thick overcoat & sat for two minutes, tears streaming out of my cold eyes and loathed the world, came back to the house – empty and cold – how I hated having written anything: so I wandered out again & shivered & longed to destroy the work of my hands – all wasted. And this was to have been the one real day in my artistic life – sympathy at the end of work.*

'World losers & world forsakers
for ever & ever.'
How true it is.

Creative life was taking on an autumnal quality with the repeated harvesting of old ideas. Early in 1913 Elgar decided to complete another project that had been with him for at least a decade. It was a 'Symphonic Study' of Shakespeare's Falstaff.

Elgar with the London Symphony Orchestra in Queen's Hall. Casting about once again for alternatives to composition, he allowed himself to be appointed the Orchestra's 'Principal Conductor' for 1911-12.

Soon after his engagements with the London Symphony Orchestra, Elgar began to make recordings for the Gramophone Company. Cramped studio arrangements and a severely reduced band were necessary for the recording of orchestral music until 1925.

Falstaff's career — like Elgar's own existence now — revolved around London. But at its centre the new score contained a West-Country pastoral. The composer himself described it:

The march, as we approach the fields and apple-trees, assumes a song-like character, until we rest in Shallow's orchard . . . with . . . some sadly-merry pipe and tabor music . . .

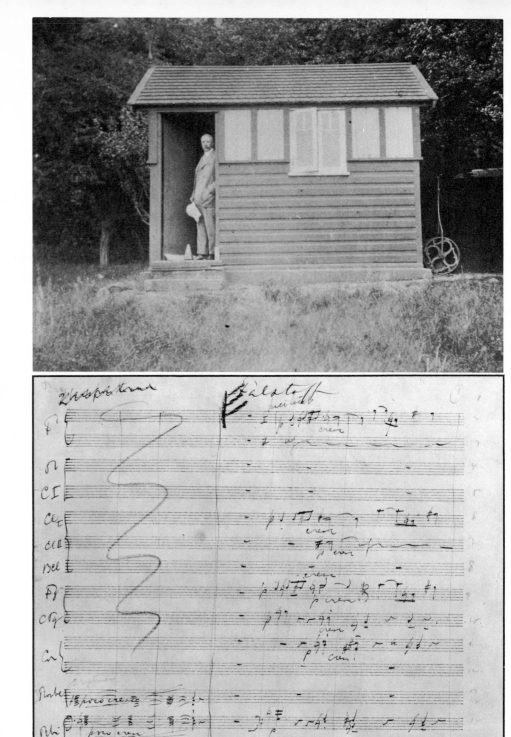

*A change of air being deemed
necessary for the composer, who
was working long hours, a
house named Tan-yr-allt
(Under the Hill) was taken at
Penmaenmawr, North Wales
[in August 1913], and here,
with the sea air blowing in
upon him from the north-west,
he settled down to the tremendous task of completing the
full score [of Falstaff].*

W. H. REED

Elgar conducted the first
performance at the Leeds
Festival in October. It was a
hollow success. The London
première a month later faced

*a beggarly row of half-empty
benches.*

ROBIN LEGGE

Between the time of *Falstaff*'s completion and its première there remained one more happy event – the Three Choirs Festival at Gloucester in September 1913. As the Festival began, Elgar had just put the final words to an essay on his new work:

Sir John Falstaff with his companions might well have said, as we may well say now,
> *'We play fools with the time, and the spirits of the wise sit in the clouds and mock us.'*

Sunday afternoon (above): Tea in Dr. Brewer's garden in the Cathedral Close after the Opening Service. Left to right: Dr. Brewer (organist of the Cathedral and the Festival conductor), W. H. Reed, Frank Schuster, Lady Elgar, Leena Lloyd, Charles Brewer, Charles Harford Lloyd, Sir Edward Elgar, Eileen Brewer, John Coates, Mrs. Brewer.

Wednesday morning (above left): On the roof of the Cathedral porch Charles Sanford Terry conducts the Festival Orchestra brass players in Elgar's arrangements of Chorales from the *St. Matthew Passion* as the audience gathers in the Close below for the Cathedral performance to follow.

Thursday afternoon (left): Charles Harford Lloyd, Herbert Brewer, Elgar, and Camille Saint-Saëns (seated), after the première of Saint-Saëns's new oratorio *The Promised Land*.

The declaration of War on 4 August 1914 found the Elgars on holiday in Scotland. They cut short their visit, but before leaving for London they saw the first Scottish troops marching away to the front.

Back at Severn House, E.E. immediately joined the Hampstead Special Constabulary.

London looks normal; it seems incredible that things shd. go on so well . . . I am a s. constable & am a 'Staff Inspector'. I am sure others cd. do the work better but none with a better will. I was equipping (serving out 'weapons'), & taking receipts & registering my men for hours last night: this morning at six I inspected the whole district — so one does what one can — It's a pity I am too old to be a soldier. I am so active.

August 1914: Sir Edward Elgar, Staff Inspector (lower left) with the Hampstead Special Constabulary.

During November Elgar was asked to contribute to an artistic
anthology to be published in aid of Belgian war charities.
After some hesitation, he found a poem by Emile Cammaerts
that suggested itself as an effective recitation against a
musical background:

'Sing, Belgians, sing . . .
Sing of the pride of our defeats
'Neath this bright Autumn sun,
And sing of the joy of honour
When cowardice might be so sweet . . .'

Carillon caught the crest of the wave of British sympathy
for the Belgian people, and its first performance on
7 December 1914 was greeted by tumultuous enthusiasm.
But for Elgar himself the War signified nothing but doom:

Everything good & nice & clean & fresh & sweet is far
away — never to return.

Near the end of 1915, in the depths of the War, Elgar wrote the music to a fantasy play for children. It was an adaptation of Algernon Blackwood's novel *A Prisoner in Fairyland*.

'O children, open your arms to me,
    Let your hair fall over my eyes;
Let me sleep a moment – and then awake
    In your garden of sweet surprise!
        For the grown-up folk
        Are a wearisome folk,
And they laugh all my fancies to scorn.'

The Starlight Express, with a delicate score by Elgar, was produced by Lena Ashwell in the Kingsway Theatre at Christmas 1915.

THE CURE FOR "WUMBLED"-NESS: WHERE THE "STAR DUST" COMES FROM

During the middle years of the War Elgar wrote a set of three brief choral works to poems by Laurence Binyon. The final one, *For the Fallen*, he dedicated

To the memory of our glorious men,
with a special thought for the Worcesters.

In March 1917 Elgar conducted a performance of *For the Fallen* in Worcester Cathedral. The Three Choirs Festivals had been suspended since 1914, and for many of the Cathedral choristers this was their first experience of singing under Elgar. One of them was the young son of the Cathedral organist Ivor Atkins:

Keyed up as we all were, the performance in the evening — in a Cathedral which was packed as I have never before or since seen it — . . . was the most moving and thrilling experience that I have ever had. War conditions precluded the use of an orchestra, and my father had to fill in as much of the orchestral colour as possible from the organ. A special platform was erected over the choir steps for the sadly depleted Worcester Festival Choral Society . . . The King's School O.T.C. supplied the drummers. Although it is over forty years ago . . . I can still feel the shivers which passed through me as the drums rolled, perhaps the contrast to organ instead of full orchestra making them even more impressive . . .

WULSTAN ATKINS

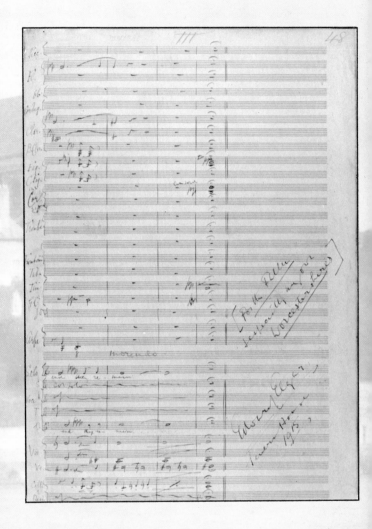

'*They shall not grow old as we that are left grow old:*
  Age shall not weary them, nor the years condemn.
At the going down of the sun and in the morning
  We will remember them.'

By 1917 his deep depression over the War was affecting Elgar's health;

I cannot do any real work with the awful shadow over us . . .

To provide a retreat for him, Alice found a remote cottage in Sussex called 'Brinkwells'. When Edward saw it he was enchanted:

. . . it's divine*: simple thatched cottage & a (soiled) studio with wonderful view: large garden unweeded, a task for 40 men.*

At Brinkwells, as the War neared its end, life seemed almost to return to the atmosphere of 1910:

I have been writing much music & I had [Billy] Reed with his violin here . . .

For one of Reed's visits, Elgar made this map.

When I arrived, Mr. Aylwyn, a neighbouring farmer, met me at the station with a pony and trap . . . We jogged along through some wonderfully wooded country, along a road which twisted and turned continually, until at last we came to about half a mile of straight road rising up a fairly steep hill, with chestnut plantations on either side. At the top of the hill, looming on the sky-line, was what at first sight I took to be a statue; but as we drew nearer I saw it was a tall woodman leaning a little forward upon an axe with a very long handle . . . It was Sir Edward himself . . . W. H. REED

At Brinkwells, during the final year of the War, Elgar finished three chamber works – his first music in many months. Then in June 1919:

I am frantically busy writing & have nearly completed a Concerto for Violoncello – a real large work & I think good & alive.

The Concerto made its way slowly at first, largely through repeated performances by Beatrice Harrison. In December 1919 she came to Severn House to prepare the work for a gramophone recording.

While they discussed interpretation, Alice tried to edit the orchestral parts for the recording. But for more than a month she had been ill:

She who had always been so full of vitality and energy was now often listless. She would creep up close to the fire and look so fragile . . .

W. H. REED

. . . she seemed to be fading away before one's very eyes.

W. H. REED

April 6th . . . I am heartbroken: our poor little dear one is inarticulate and can understand nothing. It is too awful.

The following evening she died.

The burial was in Little Malvern, close to 'Forli' and 'Craeg Lea':

The place she chose long years ago is too sweet — the blossoms are white all round & the illimitable plain, with all the hills & churches in the distance which were hers from childhood, looks just the same — inscrutable & unchanging.

Edward asked Troyte Griffith to design a gravestone:

Could the motto
*   'Fortiter et fide'*
go in: it suited dear A. so well.

Pray for the Soul of
Caroline Alice
LADY ELGAR
only Daughter of the late
Sir Henry Gee Roberts K.C.B.
of Hazeldine House
Worcestershire.
The dearly-beloved
and revered Wife
of Edward Elgar Kt.
She died at Hampstead
April 7th. 1920.
R.I.P.

All I have done was owing to her and I am at present a sad and broken man — just stunned.

After Alice s death Severn House was unbearable. In the Autumn of 1921 it was sold.

. . . I am rescuing a few papers and a few books and go forth into the world alone as I did forty-three years ago — only I am disillusioned and old.

He went to live in the centre of London:

Here I am, all alone! It is not a house, it's a flat — just sitting room, bedroom, bathroom, etc. . . .

He often took his meals at Brooks's:

I have rolled in here & am very lonely . . . so I thought — as there are only 10 footmen & 26 candlesticks of silver — I wd. write to you . . .

. . . since my dear wife's death I have done nothing & *fear my music has vanished.*

Three Choirs Festival, Hereford, 1921:

. . . he stayed with a very merry party at Brockhampton Court — the house of Colonel and Mrs. Foster. Walford Davies was there also, and between them all they managed to take him out of himself a little and to pierce the gloom which seemed to have settled upon him.

W. H. REED

Three Choirs Festival, Gloucester, 1922: (left to right) Arthur Bliss, Herbert Brewer, W. H. Reed, Sir Edward Elgar, Eugene Goossens.

The 'new music' of the post-war composers gave Elgar little personal pleasure, but he used his influence to secure invitations for Bliss and Goossens to write new works for the Three Choirs Festival. Bliss wrote to him:

I do not think you realise what a fine and rare encouragement your presence is, when, as you did at luncheon the other day you gave the lead to younger composers. It is such a unique thing, this broadminded generosity, that I hope you will be long spared to make the music of Englishmen pre-eminent.

Gloucester Cathedral,
6 September 1922: A
performance of *The
Kingdom*. Elgar, who will
conduct, stands just to
the left of the rostrum.
Herbert Brewer is on the
platform, and W. H. Reed,
leading the orchestra, is
at the left. The soloists
are (left to right): Phyllis
Lett, Agnes Nicholls, John
Coates, and Herbert
Heyner.

*He obtained all he wanted from his
executants by the movements of his
delicate and well-shaped hands, by
his eyes, which expressed the whole
gamut of emotions, and by his whole
facial expression, which lit up in an
amazing manner when he got the
response he desired and when his
music throbbed and seethed as he
intended that it should.*

W. H. REED

In 1923 Elgar returned to Worcestershire. He had found a house called
Napleton Grange, in Kempsey, and in April he moved in:

I like the name, & the village & surrounding country are to my mind.

*. . . I [feel] that I [am] no longer 'in' the world, or rather, that the old
artistic 'striving' world exists for me no more.*

Billy Reed did what he could:

*I went down there continually with my violin . . .
I would suggest that the sketch-work and scraps
belonging to Part III [of The Apostles trilogy] be
fetched out of the cupboard and played over. My violin
would come out; and I would play over his shoulder
anything suitable until I thought I had roused him
sufficiently for him to continue after I had gone away.
But nothing came of it . . .*

There were many conducting engagements, but afterwards it was always the same:

On returning to Kempsey he settled down again to the life of a country gentleman, reading a great deal, studying, and pursuing various hobbies . . .

W. H. REED

I feel like these woods all aglow — a spark wd start a flame —

— but no human spark comes.

The *Civic Fanfare*, written for the Hereford Festival in 1927, was typical of the small projects that could arouse Elgar's creative interest during the 'twenties. He conducted the première of the little work at the Opening Service on 4 September, and later in the week directed performances of *The Dream of Gerontius* and *The Music Makers*.

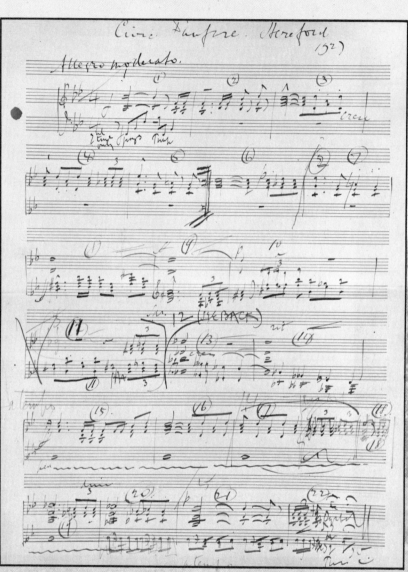

The Gramophone Company sent their mobile van to record Elgar's performances at the 1927 Hereford Festival. But there were hazards:

. . . at the Three Choir performance of Gerontius, *during a sudden silent pause after a* forte *climax, a lady's voice talking about 'a lovely camisole for 11s 6d.' was clearly exposed when the record was played back, and so ruined a fine set.*

FRED GAISBERG

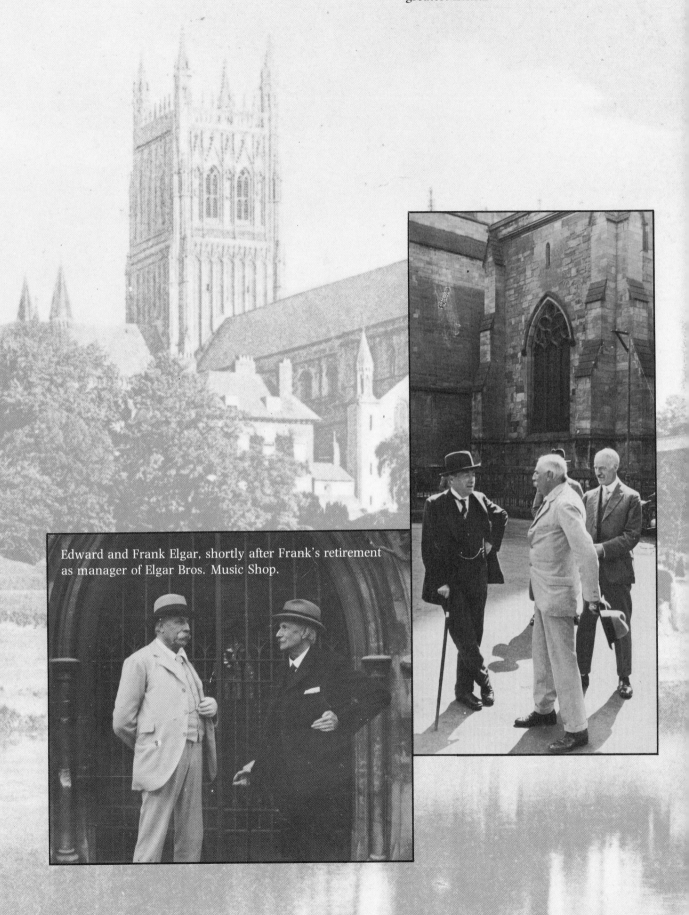

Three distinguished residents of
Worcestershire at the Cathedral:
Stanley Baldwin, the Prime Minister (left);
Sir Edward Elgar; and Sir Ivor Atkins,
the Cathedral organist and one of Elgar's
greatest friends.

Edward and Frank Elgar, shortly after Frank's retirement
as manager of Elgar Bros. Music Shop.

Kingsway Hall, London, 23 May 1931: The recording of Sir Edward's new *Nursery Suite*, 'Dedicated by permission to Their Royal Highnesses the Duchess of York and the Princesses Elizabeth and Margaret Rose.' The Duke and Duchess attended the session, together with Bernard Shaw and Sir Landon Ronald.

. . . Fred Gaisberg (artistic director of the [Gramophone] Company) handed them each a copy de luxe of the score, and we then proceeded to play it under Sir Edward's own direction. When we had played the number 'The Waggon Passes', Their Royal Highnesses' faces were wreathed in smiles and, at their request, Sir Edward repeated it.

W. H. REED

At Torquay: May 1930

In 1928 Elgar went to live for a time near Stratford:

*. . . he loved the River Avon which flowed past the end of the garden,
and bought a boat . . .*   W. H. REED

Here he was rowed by his faithful valet Dick (Richard Mountford).

At the end of 1929 Elgar came back to live in Worcester.
He purchased a house called 'Marl Bank', built on

. . . an eminence distantly overlooking the way to school
that he had taken every day as a boy sixty years before.

I bought this tiny place to be quiet.

E.E. with his daugher Carice at Marl Bank.

*Dinner at 8.30 attended by Marco . . .
& Mina . . . properly seated on chairs.
They behaved very well, patiently waiting
for morsels they would receive from Sir
E.'s hand.*

FRED GAISBERG

Sir Edward's Christmas card, 1932:
an original fable.

In a gorgeous, illimitable, golden corridor, several of the Higher-Beings were in waiting.
Around, and in mysterious depths, great and marvellous works were making. . . .

But the New World, it seemed, was not going well.
' I do not see why a New World,' said Gabriel.
Uriel surveyed, with hesitating discontent, a trumpet.
' Have you to play that thing ? ' asked Raphael.
' Some day,' Uriel answered, without enthusiasm. . . .
A vast Purple Shadow filled the space and Lucifer sat. Ithuriel slightly shifted his spear.
' How,' asked One, ' do you, Intellect, picture what is coming ? '
Lucifer answered,—' I shall like it ; there will be much to amuse besides the religions.'
' Nonsense,' said Gabriel, ' they are dull.'
' Also,' continued the Purple One with considerable relish, ' I shall enjoy Shakespeare ; he will
say I am a gentleman. Milton—'
' We are sick of Milton,' hastily interrupted the Others,—' of Milton and a whole lot of
insufferable bores. Why, oh why, must it be ? ' . . .

Michael fingered a sword and saw his effigy as the everlasting maître d'armes ; Raphael groaned,
' Think of me in pictures of that wretched boy with his eternal fish ! '
Uriel, Ithuriel and the rest yawned, ' Unhappy Earth, why, oh why ? ' . . .

From somewhere near came a curiously pleasant sound ; pleasant and not unmirthful.
If the MAKER-OF-ALL could be pleased beyond ordinary with any single piece of work, it
would seem that the last created thing was of an excellence surpassing those grisly gewgaws which
HE had seen and found good. . . .

Michael drew the draped curtain ; then backed away, radiant.
' HE is pleased,—HE laughs,—HE has made, (Michael whispered) —a Puppy ! '
The august features of the Higher-Beings relaxed. ' The Earth is well,' they chanted, ' a Puppy ! '

The Purple Shade heaved outward and sank below.
Lucifer knew that through the ages Man could be serenely happy with his DOG.

Marl Bank is not very far from Malvern; and G.B.S. frequently came over to see him when he was staying there for the annual Drama Festival . . . He had, in fact, asked Shaw to write an opera libretto for him. Shaw replied that his plays set themselves to a verbal music of their own which would make a very queer sort of counterpoint with Elgar's music. . . [But] Sir Edward was stage-struck and wanted to play at opera-making. He therefore called in another Malvern friend, Sir Barry Jackson, who indulged the new fancy in the most sympathetic and helpful way.

W. H. REED

. . . Elgar was very headstrong and not a little difficult when he had conceived a situation on the stage in a certain way . . . [He] would alter an idea here in deference to Barry's judgment, perhaps; but he would fight for an idea there until he had convinced Barry that it was practicable.

W. H. REED

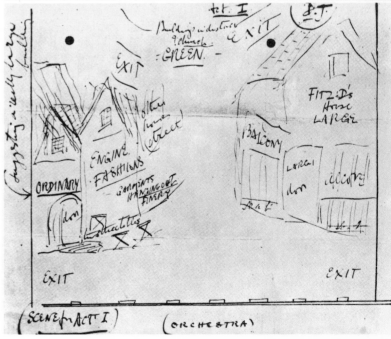

. . . he would tell the story of the opera with a wealth of detail . . . Seizing a piece of paper during one of these discussions he hurriedly drew in pen and ink a rough sketch of the stage showing the position of the church, the green, exits and entrances. He seemed to have it all in his head.

W. H. REED

. . . I had a great ambition to have Sir Edward himself conduct [a recording of the Violin Concerto]. As a youthful and pliant performer without prejudice, who would respond best to his instruction, I selected Yehudi Menuhin as the most promising soloist . . The Spring of 1932 brought the Menuhin family to London, where frequent meetings between the great composer and his young admirer took place. Yehudi's fresh, agile mind, so quick to grasp the instructions, drew from Sir Edward high praise and encouragement . . .

FRED GAISBERG

14 July 1932: Yehudi Menuhin and Sir Edward Elgar at the Gramophone Company's London studios for the recording of the *Violin Concerto*.

. . . they were . . . widening the bridge over his beloved Severn: the old familiar bridge he had known all his life . . . He could not bear to part with the old iron balustrades . . . that were being removed; so he bought two lengths of them and had them brought up on lorries to Marl Bank and set up there . . . in the garden . . . I think he used to go out and imagine that the Severn was flowing under them as of old.

W. H. REED

When the Menuhins arranged a performance of the *Violin Concerto* in Paris, Elgar decided to fly. While in France he called upon Delius, who asked him what flying was like. Elgar replied:

Well, to put it poetically, it is not unlike your life and my life. The rising from the ground was a little difficult; you cannot tell exactly how you are going to stand it. When once you have reached the heights it is very different. There is a delightful feeling of elation in sailing through gold and silver clouds. It is, Delius, rather like your music — a little intangible sometimes, but always very beautiful. I should have liked to stay there for ever. The descent is like our old age — peaceful, even serene.

In June 1932 Elgar reached his seventy-fifth birthday. For more than a dozen years he had written no major work. But now the B.B.C., at the suggestion of Bernard Shaw, made a formal request for his Third Symphony:

Elgar accepted the commission, and indeed began to write sketches and fragments in his usual way to the great joy of his friends and admirers, who had visions of a great new work materialising at last. The opening of 1933 found him busy writing and sketching . . .

W. H. REED

*In the latter part of 1933 he began to get all these fragments —
in some instances as many as twenty or thirty consecutive
bars — on paper, though they were rarely harmonically
complete. A clear vision of the whole Symphony was forming
in his mind.*

W. H. REED

*. . . but I never could find out how it was to end. Whenever I
asked the question he always became mysterious and vague,
and said,*

    'Ah, that we shall see.'

W. H. REED

He continued working at his opera and the Third Symphony until
September, when he went to Hereford to conduct his works at the Three
Choirs Festival . . .

W. H. REED

Hereford Cathedral, 2.50 p.m. Sunday, 3 September 1933. Sir Edward Elgar opens the Three Choirs Festival by conducting the London Symphony Orchestra in his *Imperial March* – written for the Diamond Jubilee of Queen Victoria in 1897 – and the *Civic Fanfare* composed for the Hereford Festival thirty years later. Sir Edward conducts quietly from his seat, his snow-white hair contrasting with the black velvet of full court dress, the scarlet robes of the Oxford doctorate put off momentarily at his back.

Elgar, his daughter, one of his nieces, Harriet Cohen,
Herbert Sumsion and I were having tea in the garden
of a house in Hereford which Elgar had taken for the
festival week. The festival and perhaps the golden sunlight
of that evening had induced in Elgar a remembering
mood. While we were listening to his eager, nervous, yet
quiet-toned voice we saw Mrs. Bernard Shaw and then
her husband coming through the gate [from the Cathedral,
where they had just attended the performance of
Mendelssohn's Elijah].

'We were hoping that we were not too late for tea,'
said Shaw from the distance.

'No, no. Come along. Very glad to see you,' and
within a minute the two were engaged in an intent
dialogue . . .

'Now, now, Shaw,' Elgar was saying . . . 'I can't pass
that,' for, in discussing the performance of Elijah, Shaw
had declared that the trouble with Mendelssohn was that
he couldn't orchestrate.

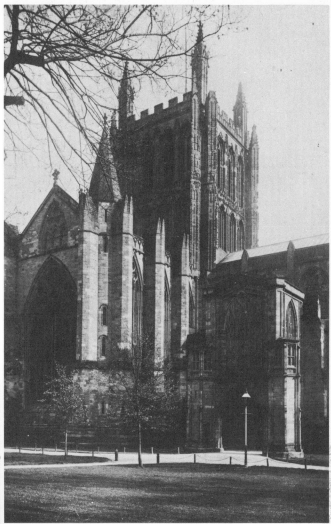

Elgar . . . took the big, awkward volume [of the full
score], spread it open on his knees and . . .

'There's a good stroke,' Elgar exclaimed. 'There's
another. And my word, look here. D'you see?'

As page after page of contrary evidence was shown him,
Bernard Shaw laughed to think that he could have been
so mistaken . . .

BASIL MAINE

That evening Elgar conducted *The Dream of Gerontius*
in the Cathedral. It was the last time.

I said to Elgar: 'What do you think about this folk music?'
He flashed back: 'I don't think about it at all. I am folk music!'

TROYTE GRIFFITH

. . . he did not move about very much or seem to want to go for walks as before. He sat mostly in that pleasant garden receiving and entertaining his friends . . .

W. H. REED

After the Festival . . . I was startled to hear that he was to undergo some small operation and was going into a nursing-home for it at once. The next thing I heard was that the operation had taken place; that it was far more serious than had at first been supposed . . . W. H. REED

The gramophone played a great role in his life at this time and for five months was his chief consolation . . . He had a whim in December to have himself photographed, and to the nursing home one day I brought a photographer . . . FRED GAISBERG

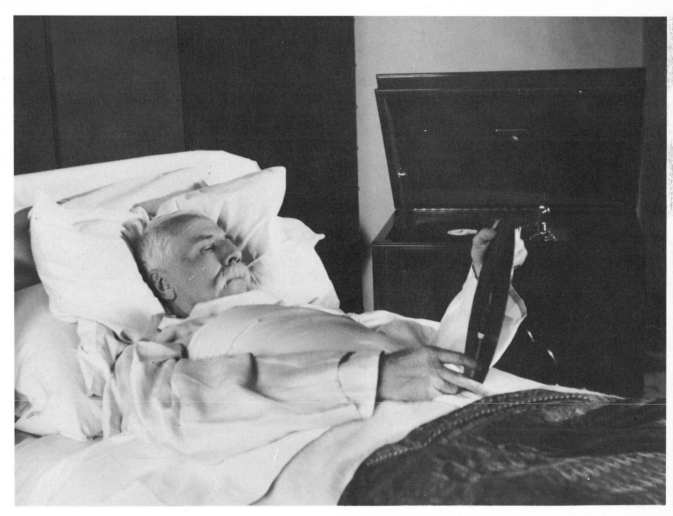

. . . during his . . . illness I put the Stratton Quartet's records of his String Quartet on the gramophone.
After the Slow movement I said, 'Surely that is as fine as a movement by Beethoven.'
He said quite simply, 'Yes it is, and there is something in it that has never been done before.'
I said, 'What is it?'
He answered, 'Nothing you would understand, merely an arrangement of notes.'

TROYTE GRIFFITH

*. . . it was pitiful to see him receding, fading away from us all
so certainly that there was no doubt about the hopelessness
of his illness.*

W. H. REED

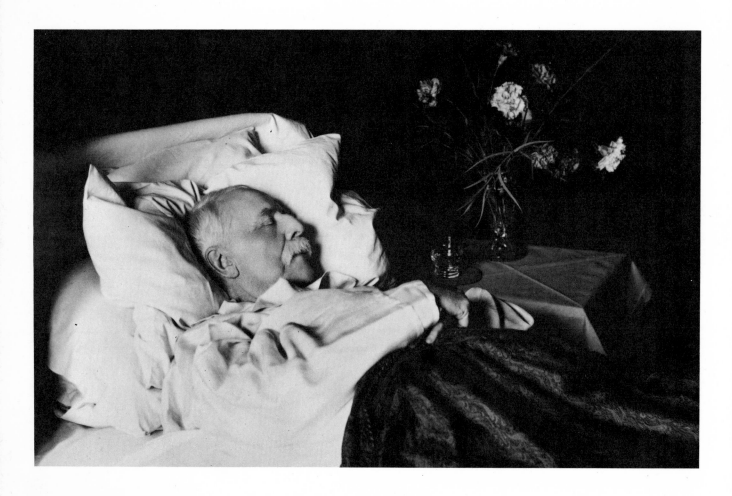

*I sat watching him for some time, noting his familiar features
which had scarcely changed at all during his illness; his hair
was a little whiter perhaps, and his characteristic nose with
its high bridge was a trifle more prominent, but his colour
was good, and he did not look very much thinner than before . . .
He suddenly opened his eyes . . . looking intently into my
face for a few seconds . . . and putting out his hand, let it
rest on mine, and drew me a little nearer . . .*

*'. . . the Symphony . . . all bits and pieces . . . no one would
understand . . . no one . . . no one . . . I think you had better
burn it.'*

W. H. REED

One day when the pain left him a little he asked for a pencil
and a piece of music paper, and as he lay there he wrote what
was probably in his head as the end of his Third Symphony —
or perhaps he meant it to represent the end of his life's work.

The following day [I] was again with him and he fumbled
about in his pillow for a little without saying anything.
Presently he found what he sought and handed these four bars
of music to [me], fighting back the tears which were choking
him as he said:

'Billy, this is the end.'

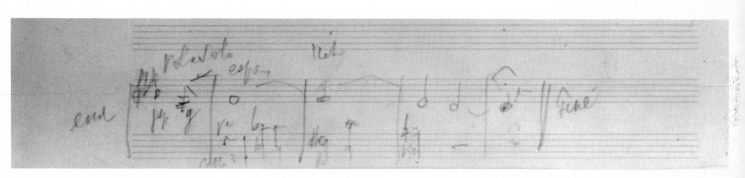

This fragment is the very last music he put on paper. After
making this effort he seemed to fade gradually away from day
to day. At the end his pain left him and he died peacefully
on 23rd February 1934.

W. H. REED

Postscript

A perception of time and place can often aid understanding. Perhaps a purely visual experience cannot offer any direct explication of music. But what these photographs may suggest is something of the creative attitude itself. For a vision of an artist's world is less a documenting of places and events than a half-promise of confronting — perhaps at alarmingly close quarters — the very act of creation.

The life depicted in these pages was one for which I came too late to enter in any direct way. For that reason I owe a particular debt of gratitude to the men and women whose friendship I have been privileged to share with Elgar himself: Carice Elgar Blake, May and Madeline Grafton, Lady Bantock, Sir Barry Jackson, Agnes Nicholls (Lady Harty), Mrs. Helen Goodman, Beatrice and Margaret Harrison, Dora Powell, Sir Percy and Lady Hull, Harriet Cohen, Dr. Herbert Howells, Marjorie Ffrangcon Davies, Charles Brewer, Col. and Mrs. Philip Leicester, Lilian Griffith, Astra Desmond, E. Wulstan Atkins, Rutland Boughton, Francis Reed, Mr. and Mrs. Alan Webb, Isabella Wallich, Yehudi Menuhin. Their remembered experiences have deeply influenced the making of this book. Some of these, and a few other friends, have helped to guide its growth over the number of years it has required.

One cannot experiment in a protracted way with any historical material, however, without discovering its almost volatile responsiveness to one's own desires. Inevitably these pages have shaped themselves as a personal essay; and thus there are two other 'friends pictured within' whose influence will have been at least as profound as any other. They are my parents, to whom I would dedicate the book.

JERROLD NORTHROP MOORE
Hampstead, July 1971.

Sources of photographs and quotations

Reproduced by kind permission of the copyright owners wherever it has been possible to establish them. Grateful thanks are due to the trustees of the Elgar Birthplace, and to the Elgar Will Trust for permission to reproduce photographs and manuscripts in their possession. Unless otherwise stated, the music quoted from published works is the copyright of Novello and Company Ltd.

A name in parentheses following the photographer indicates the fact that the picture has been rephotographed for this book. In all other cases the printer has worked from a positive print secured directly from the original negative.

page

2. Anonymous postcard photograph, postmarked 1906.
4. Engraving by W. & J. Walker from a drawing by E. F. Burney. (Published 1 November 1792 by Harrison & Co., 18, Paternoster Row, London).
5. West Country landscape. Photographed by W. A. Call, Monmouth.
   Worcester c. 1860. Anonymous photograph in Worcestershire Record Office (Michael Dowty).
   Friar Street. Postcard photography by F. Frith & Co., Reigate.
6. Elgar Bros. Music Shop. Photograph by W. Harris (M. Dowty).
   W. H. Elgar. Anonymous photograph.
   'Old E. always handed round . . .' Hubert or Philip Leicester, quoted in *Edward Elgar*, by Diana McVeagh (London: J. M. Dent & Sons, 1955), p. 3.
   'I shut him up . . .' Letter to C. W. Buck, 7.x.85. *Letters of Edward Elgar*, ed. Percy M. Young (London: Geoffrey Bles, 1956), p. 19.
7. At Old Hills. Anonymous postcard photograph.
   'Only a sprig of heather . . .' Quoted in *Elgar O.M.*, by Percy M. Young (London: Collins, 1955), p. 28.
   Anne Elgar. Photograph by George Evans, Tallow Hill, Worcester.
   'Our Mother was romantic . . .' MS. by Lucy Elgar, 1912, at the Elgar Birthplace.
8. Malvern Hills. Anonymous photograph, c. 1930.
   Elgar Birthplace. Drawing, c. 1850. Photograph by Foy, Worcester.
   'How well I remember . . .' MS by Lucy Elgar, 1912, at the Elgar Birthplace.
   Edward and his mother. Anonymous daguerreotype photograph.
9. 'I saw and learnt . . .' Interview with Dr. Edward Elgar, by Rupert de Cordova, *Strand Magazine*, May 1904, pp. 538-9.
   'Our walk was always . . .' Preface by Elgar to *Forgotten Worcester*, by Hubert A. Leicester (Worcester: Ebenezer Baylis, 1930), pp. 10-11.
   Worcester High Street and Cathedral. Postcard photograph.
   The Severn near the Cathedral steps. Photograph by Michael Dowty, May 1971.
10. Anne Elgar's couplets, written 12.xi.74. MS in possession of the late Miss Madeline Grafton, Wetherby, Yorks.
    Harry Elgar. Photograph by C. R. Pettinger, Cheltenham.
    Lucy Elgar. Anonymous photograph.
    Polly Elgar. Photograph by Norman May, Worcester.
11. Joseph and Edward Elgar. Photograph by George Evans.
    'He was called . . .' MS by Lucy Elgar, 1912, at the Elgar Birthplace.
    Frank Elgar. Photograph by George Evans.
    Helen Elgar. Photograph by George Evans.
12. The Severn at the Old Water-works, Worcester. Anonymous postcard photograph, postmarked 1906.
    'I am still at heart . . .' Letter to Sidney Colvin, 13.xii.21. Worcestershire Record Office.
    'By means of a stage-allegory . . .' 'The Wand of Youth: a note by the composer,' in 'His Master's Voice' Album 80, 1929.
    'Our orchestral means . . .' Typescript note on *The Wand of Youth*, Second Suite, 'Written by E.E. at Hereford'. Elgar Birthplace.

page

'. . . the bass consist[ed] . . .' 'The Wand of Youth: a note by the composer,' in 'His Master's Voice' Album 80, 1929.
The Elgar children in 1868. Anonymous photograph (M. Dowty).
13. Edward at the age of eleven. Photograph by George Evans.
    Claines Churchyard. Photograph by Michael Dowty, May 1971.
    'Nervous, sensitive & kind . . .' MS in possession of the late Miss Madeline Grafton.
    'In studying scores . . .' *Strand* interview, p. 540.
    '. . . a most miserable-looking lad . . .' Hubert Leicester, quoted in *Edward Elgar*, by D. McVeagh, p. 6.
14. Edward at about fourteen. Photograph by T. Bennett (M. Dowty).
    'When I resolved . . .' *Strand* interview, pp. 538-9.
    '. . . I am self-taught . . .' *Strand* interview, p. 539.
    'I told my mother . . .' Recollection by Sir Compton Mackenzie, in *The Fifteenth Variation*, B.B.C. broadcast, 1957.
    Catel treatise (Elgar's copy). Photograph by M. Dowty.
    Mozart treatise (Elgar's copy). Photograph by M. Dowty.
15. 'I attended as many . . .' *Strand* interview, p. 539.
    Worcester Cathedral. Postcard photograph, c. 1910.
    St. George's Catholic Church, Worcester. Postcard photograph (G. Hopcraft).
    '1872 July 14 . . .' quoted in *Portrait of Elgar*, by M. Kennedy, p. 8.
    The wind quintet. Photograph by T. Bennett.
    '. . . five of us . . .' *Strand* interview, p. 540.
16. '. . . many new works were produced . . .' 'An essay on the gramophone' by Sir Edward Elgar, in *An Elgar Discography*, by Jerrold Northrop Moore (London: British Institute of Recorded Sound, 1963), p. iv.
    '. . . he always spoke . . .' *Elgar as I knew him*, by W. H. Reed (London: Victor Gollancz Ltd., 1936), pp. 46-7.
    Crystal Palace. Valentine postcard photograph.
    Symphony score. Photograph by M. Dowty.
    Edward at about twenty-one. Photograph by Vanderweyde, London.
    '[In 1878] I . . . ruled a score . . .' *Strand* interview, p. 539.
17. 'Then I began to teach . . .' *Strand* interview, p. 538.
    Elgar with violin. Anonymous photograph.
    Powick Asylum. Anonymous photograph (G. Hopcraft).
    Programme of 14 March 1882. Photographs by M. Dowty.
18. Malvern. Peacock postcard photograph.
    Announcement of Elgar's teaching in Malvern. Photograph by M. Dowty.
    'I showed it to old Stockley . . .' Letter to C. W. Buck, 8.i.86. *Letters of Edward Elgar*, p. 23.
    Elgar at about twenty-five. Anonymous photograph.
    '. . . a spare, dark, shy young man . . .' Letter from A. B. L– W. to the *Henley and South Oxfordshire Standard*, 30.iii.34.
19. 'He took a room in Malvern . . .' 'My memories of my father', by Carice Elgar Blake, in *Music and Musicians*, June 1957, p. 11.
    Caroline Alice Roberts. Photograph by Schemboche, c. 1885.

page

Hazeldine House. Postcard photograph by Alfred W. S. Tozer, Redmarley.
20. '. . . I must tell you . . .' Letter to C. W. Buck, 6.x.89. *Letters of Edward Elgar*, p. 46.
    Mr. and Mrs. Elgar. Photograph by B. Johannes, Garmisch, probably 1892.
    51, Avonmore Road, West Kensington. Photograph by G. G. Hodgkins, 1970.
    Worcester across the fields. Photograph by W. A. Call, Monmouth.
    Froissart Overture MS full score. Photograph by G. Hopcraft.
21. 'Sinclair pointed Elgar out to me . . .' quoted in 'Music in the provinces: the Elgar-Atkins letters', by Wulstan Atkins, in Proceedings of the *Royal Musical Association*, 1957-8, pp. 28-9.
    '. . . the fogs here are terrifying . . .' Letter to Frank Webb, 8.ii.91. *Letters of Edward Elgar*, p. 51.
    'Dec. 30. A thought this . . .' Elgar family diary, quoted in *Elgar O.M.*, by P. Young, p. 65.
22. Malvern Link and Common. Postcard photograph by Tilley & Son, Ledbury.
    'The violin lessons . . .' *Edward Elgar: the Record of a Friendship*, by Rosa Burley and Frank C. Carruthers (London: Barrie & Jenkins, 1972), p. 21.
    'Teaching was like . . .' Quoted in *Elgar: his life and works*, by Basil Maine (London: G. Bell & Sons Ltd., 1933) Life, p. 69.
    The Elgars at 'Forli'. Anonymous photograph.
    The Mount School, Malvern. Photograph by Michael Dowty, 1972.
    '. . . One day after the ensemble practice . . .' *Edward Elgar: the record of a friendship*, by Burley and Carruthers, p. 38.
23. '. . . Carice is a most wonderfully lovely infant . . .' Letter to C. W. Buck, 20.xii.91. *Letters of Edward Elgar*, p. 54.
    Alice with Carice. Anonymous photograph, c. 1892.
    'I *don't* like doing it . . .' Letter to Frank Webb, 29.xi.89. *Letters of Edward Elgar*, p. 47.
    Serenade, arranged for piano duet, MS score. British Museum photograph.
    Edward golfing at Stoke Prior. Photograph by William Grafton, c. 1893. The two background figures are May Grafton and Frank Elgar.
    'Golf – call it a game . . .' Untitled, undated single sheet of typescript now at the Elgar Birthplace.
24. The Bavarian Highlands. Anonymous souvenir photograph brought back from an excursion by the Elgars during the 1890's.
    '. . . there are large pine forests . . .' Letter to the Grafton children, 2.viii.92. *Letters of Edward Elgar*, pp. 57-8.
    'fired with songs' Elgar family diary, quoted in *Elgar O.M.*, by P. Young, p. 69.
    Scenes from the Bavarian Highlands: Lullaby 'In Hammersbach', MS full score. British Museum photograph.
25. 'Wordmonger' cartoon. Photograph by D. Tripp.
    'She gave up . . .' 'A family retrospect', by Carice Elgar Blake, in *Edward Elgar Centenary Sketches* (London: Novello & Co., 1957), p. 6.
    'The care of a genius . . .' Elgar family diary, 1914, quoted in *Elgar O.M.*, by P. Young, p. 169.
    Caroline Alice Elgar. Photograph by Claud Harris, c. 1912.

page

26. '. . . we stood at the door . . .' Letter from Anne Elgar to Polly Grafton, 11.xii.98, quoted in *Elgar O.M.*, by P. Young, p. 81.
Elgar in the Malvern Hills. Anonymous photograph.
The British Camp from Birchwood. Photograph by Alan Webb, 1933.
Caractacus: Woodland Interlude MS full score. Novello & Co. photograph.

27. Mr. and Mrs. W. H. Elgar, *c*. 1900. Photograph by May Grafton.
'. . . what can I say to him . . .' Letter from Anne Elgar to Alice Elgar, 23.vi.02. Quoted in *Elgar O.M.*, by P. Young, p. 105.

28. C.A.E. Photograph by Reginald Haines.
H.D.S-P. Anonymous photograph.
B.G.N. Anonymous photograph.
R.B.T. Anonymous photograph.
W.M.B. Anonymous photograph.
R.P.A. Anonymous photograph.
Ysobel. Anonymous photograph.
Troyte. Anonymous photograph.
Theme 'Enigma' MS full score. British Museum photograph.

29. 'One evening . . .' quoted in *Elgar: his life and works*, by B. Maine. Works, p. 101.
'. . . I've written the variations . . .' Letter to A. J. Jaeger, 24.x.98, Elgar Birthplace.
'I heard yesterday . . .' quoted in *Myself and others*, by Sir Landon Ronald (London: Sampson, Low, Marston & Co. Ltd., n.d. [*c*. 1931]), p. 154.
W.N. Anonymous photograph.
Nimrod. Photograph by E. T. Holding.
Dorabella. Anonymous photograph.
G.R.S. and Dan. Photograph by Gus Edwards, 1896 (D. Tripp).
B.G.N. Anonymous photograph.
Lady Mary Lygon. Anonymous photograph, Edinburgh.
E.D.U. Photograph by Max Mossel, 1896 (D. Tripp).

30. 'Craeg Lea'. Photograph by F. Frith & Co., Reigate (M. Dowty).
Great Malvern and the Vale of Evesham from Beacon Hill. Peacock postcard photograph, postmarked 1904.
'A country life . . .' *Strand* interview, p. 544.
Elgar with his bicycle. Anonymous photograph.
'There cannot have been a lane . . .' *Edward Elgar: the record of a friendship*, by Burley and Carruthers, p. 145.
Edward and Carice. Photograph by William Eller, 3.viii.00.
'She was a dear little girl . . .' *Memories of a variation*, by Mrs. Richard Powell (Methuen & Co. Ltd., London, 1949), p. 11.

31. *The Dream of Gerontius* short score. Photograph by M. Dowty.
'The poem has been soaking in my mind . . .' quoted in 'Edward Elgar', [by A. J. Jaeger] in *The Musical Times*, 1.x.00, p. 648.

32. The Elgars at Birchwood Lodge. Photograph by S. Jebb Scott.
'. . . the trees are singing my music . . .' Letter to A. J. Jaeger, 11.vii.00. Elgar Birthplace.
'. . . I cycled over from Ledbury . . .' Quoted in *The Music Student*, August 1916, p. 350.

33-35. *The Dream of Gerontius* MS full score. Photographs by F. R. Logan, Birmingham.

33. Elgar finishing the score of *Gerontius*. Photograph by William Eller, 3.viii.00.

34. 'Elgar was alongside Richter . . .' MS of W. T. Edgley, 1950, quoted in *Edward Elgar*, by D. McVeagh, pp. 30-1.
Elgar in the garden of The Mount, Malvern, 29.ix.00. Anonymous photograph.

35. *Gerontius* conducted by Richter at the Birmingham Festival, 1909. Birmingham Weekly Post photograph.
'I have worked hard . . .' Letter to A. J. Jaeger, 9.x.00. Elgar Birthplace.

36. The Guildhall, London. Anonymous postcard photograph.
'Cockaigne was suggested to me . . .' fragmentary

MS entitled 'The question of programme music'. Elgar Birthplace.
Cockaigne Overture MS full score. British Museum photograph. Copyright Boosey & Co. Ltd.

37. Ivy Scar Rock, Malvern Hills. Postcard photograph by Tilley & Son, Ledbury.
Cockaigne cover design by Patten Wilson. Photograph by G. Hopcraft.
Elgar in the study at 'Craeg Lea'. Anonymous photograph.
'. . . it has taught me . . .' Letter to Hans Richter, 25.x.01, quoted in *Portrait of Elgar*, by M. Kennedy, pp. 175-6.

38. Caricature of Elgar by Ernest Forbes. Photograph by D. Tripp.
'I've got a tune . . .' *Memories of a variation*, by Mrs. Powell, p. 35.
'A tune like that . . .' quoted in *Elgar O.M.*, by P. Young, p. 289.
'The people simply rose and yelled . . .' *My life of music*, by Sir Henry Wood (London: Victor Gollancz Ltd., 1946), p. 154.
Pomp and Circumstance March no. 1 MS full score. British Museum photograph. Copyright Boosey & Co. Ltd.

39. 'We boys were in the garden . . .' A son of W. M. Baker, quoted in *Memories of a variation*, by Mrs. Powell, p. 102.
Gloucester Cathedral. Anonymous postcard photograph.
'Nanty Ewart' at Hasfield Court. Photograph by Harold Wintle, ix.01.
'Nanty Ewart' letter. Photograph by D. Tripp.
'After the duel'. Photograph by Harold Wintle, ix.01.

40. Commemorative Elgar card. Wrench & Co.
Garden of the Concert Hall, Dusseldorf. Postcard photograph.
'I drink to the welfare . . .' quoted in *Portrait of Elgar*, by M. Kennedy, p. 100.
Richard Strauss. Anonymous photograph, presented to Elgar 1904.

41. *Coronation Ode* programme. Photograph by E. diCusati.
Bredon, Worcestershire. Burrow postcard photograph, postmarked 1903.
'People were already going up . . .' Rosa Burley, quoted in *Letters to Nimrod*, ed. Percy M. Young (London: Dennis Dobson, 1965), p. 165.
'Don't for heaven's sake, *sympathise* . . .' Letter to A. J. Jaeger, 24.vi.02. Worcestershire Record Office 705:445:8543.

42. 'The Apostles were young men . . .' Francis Reeve, quoted in *Sir Edward Elgar*, by Robert J. Buckley (London: John Lane – The Bodley Head, 1905), p. 8.
Elgar in 1903. Photograph by Dr. Charles F. Grindrod.

42-43. *The Apostles*: 'By the Wayside' MS full score. British Museum photographs.

43. 'Christ in the wilderness', by Kramskoi. Photograph of the engraving in Elgar's possession, probably by May Grafton.
'Here he used to sit and dream . . .' *Elgar as I knew him*, by W. H. Reed, p. 99.
Longdon Marsh. Photograph by Dr. Charles F. Grindrod, *c*. 1903.

44-45. *The Sketch* photographic interview.

46. Elgar in Italy, 1903-04. Anonymous photograph.
'. . . one step outside the door . . .' Letter to A. J. Jaeger, 3.i.04. Worcestershire Record Office 705:445:8676.

46-47. Three Italian scenes. Photographs by Edward Elgar. 1903-04.

47. 'Alassio. Jan 3 1904 . . .' Letter to A. J. Jaeger. Worcestershire Record Office 705:445:8676.
In the South Overture. Novello & Co. printed score. Photograph by M. Dowty.
'Bedlam' – Letter from A. J. Jaeger to Elgar, 4.iii.04. Worcestershire Record Office 705:445:8718.
'. . . try as we will . . .' Letter from A. J. Jaeger to Elgar, 1.iii.04. Worcestershire Record Office, 705:445:8716.

48. 'I wish you could have seen E . . .' Letter from Alice Elgar to Polly Grafton, 17.iii.04. Worcestershire Record Office 705:684:BA5664.
Covent Garden Elgar Festival poster. Photograph by Michael Dowty.
'. . . dear little Mrs. E . . .' Letter from A. J. Jaeger to Dora Penny, 27.iii.04, quoted in *Memories of a variation*, by Mrs. Powell, p. 60.
'. . . he & E. had much talk.' Letter from Alice Elgar to Polly Grafton, 22.iii.04. Worcestershire Record Office 705:684:BA5664.

49. 'A. told E. of letter . . .' Elgar family diary, quoted in *Elgar O.M.*, by P. Young, p. 114.
W. H. Elgar and Edward. Photograph by May Grafton, 23.vi.04.
'How good of you to go . . .' Letter of Helen Elgar (Sister Mary Reginald) to Edward Elgar, 25.vi.04, quoted in *Elgar O.M.*, by P. Young, p. 114.
'The King smiled charmingly . . .' Elgar family diary, quoted in *Elgar O.M.*, by P. Young, p. 114.
King Edward VII. Rotary photograph.

50. '. . . we are almost certainly leaving here . . .' Letter to A. J. Jaeger, 29.viii.03. Worcestershire Record Office 705:445:8607.
Hereford. Photochron postcard photograph, postmarked 1933.
'Plas Gwyn'. Photograph by May Grafton, *c*. 1905.
'I think *great* music can be written here . . .' *Memories of a variation*, by Mrs. Powell, p. 63.

51. 'Plas Gwyn' with Elgar on the veranda. Photograph by May Grafton.
Alice Elgar at the sundial. Photograph by Percy Hull 20.ix.10.
Carice with Peter Rabbit. Photograph by May Grafton, *c*. 1907.
'To Carice'. MS at Elgar Birthplace.

52. 'Some three years ago . . .' Note written by Elgar in January 1905 for the first performance of the *Introduction and Allegro*.
Ynys Lochtyn, Llangranog. Postcard photograph by Judge's Ltd.
Introduction and Allegro MS full score. British Museum photograph.
The Wye River. Photograph by W. A. Call, Monmouth, *c*. 1905.
'The sketch was forgotten . . .' Note by Elgar for the first performance of the *Introduction and Allegro*.

53. 'How and when do I do my music? . . .' *Strand* interview, p. 544.
The study at 'Plas Gwyn'. Composite photograph by May Grafton.
'The composer wrote at a table . . .' and 'I once watched him . . .' *Memories of a variation*, by Mrs. Powell, p. 127.
Elgar in the study at 'Plas Gwyn'. Photograph by May Grafton.
'Plas Gwyn' study with piano. Photograph by May Grafton.
'There is one point . . .' Sir Edward Elgar at home: a 'Music Student' chat with the composer [by Percy Scholes], in *The Music Student*, August 1916, p. 343.

54. W. H. Elgar at no. 10, High Street. Photograph by May Grafton, 12.ix.05.
The Guildhall, Worcester. Postcard photograph by F. Frith & Co., Reigate.
The civic procession leaving the Guildhall. Anonymous photograph, 12.ix.05.
'[I] well remember . . .' *Elgar*, by W. H. Reed (London: J. M. Dent and Sons Ltd., 1946), p. 87.

55. The University of Birmingham. Postcard photograph, *c*. 1905.
Poster for Elgar's inaugural lecture. Photograph by M. Dowty.
'A retrospect' Lecture MS. Photograph by G. Hopcraft.
'I hold that the Symphony . . .' '*A Future for English Music*' and other lectures, by Edward Elgar, ed. Percy M. Young (London: Dennis Dobson, 1968), p. 207'

Oxford University Press, Ely House, London W. 1

GLASGOW   NEW YORK   TORONTO   MELBOURNE   WELLINGTON
CAPE TOWN   IBADAN   NAIROBI   DAR ES SALAAM   LUSAKA   ADDIS   ABABA
DELHI   BOMBAY   CALCUTTA   MADRAS   KARACHI   LAHORE   DACCA
KUALA LUMPUR   SINGAPORE   HONG KONG   TOKYO

ISBN 0 19 315425 0

© Oxford University Press

Designer: Roger Davies

First published 1973
Second impression 1974

Set in Monophoto Photina by Filmtype Services Limited, Scarborough. Reproduction by Colourcraftsmen, Chelmsford. Printed in Great Britain by A.B.C. Printers, Storrington.